LIFE AFTER BEEF:

REFLECTIONS OF A VEGETARIAN

Les Inglis

Cabbage Palm Press
Osprey, FL 34229

LIFE AFTER BEEF: Reflections of a Vegetarian

) 0/ ∞

"Somewhere a Heart Beats" by Betty Jahn
Reprinted with permission.

Printed in the United States of America
10 9 8 7 6 5 4 3 2 1

Published by:
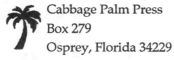 Cabbage Palm Press
Box 279
Osprey, Florida 34229

Library of Congress Catalog Card Number: 91-77295

ISBN: 0-9631496-0-1

To Charlene

Partner in life and lifestyle

TABLE OF CONTENTS

Foreword by Dr. Michael W. Fox
Preface

SECTION ONE — GETTING STARTED

SECTION TWO —GOING WAY BACK

SECTION THREE —VEGETARIAN LIFE

SECTION FOUR —HEALTH

SECTION FIVE —ANIMALS AND HUNTING

SECTION SIX — ENVIRONMENT

SECTION SEVEN —A FINAL WORD

Foreword

It gives me great pleasure to write this foreword for an author whom I regard as a kindred spirit. He has served as a member of the board of directors of the Humane Society of the United States for a few years during which time I have come to deeply respect his concern, wisdom and sincerity. By coincidence, I started to write this foreword at the United Nations in New York just prior to participating in the inauguration of the World Sustainable Agriculture Association. To go from the highly personal dimension of *Life After Beef* to the global vision of a humane, socially just and sustainable agriculture is an easy step. It is an easy step because a balanced diet, low in animal fat and protein, or even lacking such ingredients, is good for one's health and for the health of the planet.

Eating and living with conscience reconnects person and planet in such an intimate way when one realizes the connection between high animal fat and protein consumption and the environmentally harmful consequences of raising animals primarily for human consumption. The natural world cannot sustain a human population of 5.3 billion and a livestock population of over 4 billion, except at great cost to wildlife through loss of habitat and biodiversity. Until the livestock population is integrated with ecologically sound and sustainable farming practices, and until people, especially in the developed world, begin to eat and live with conscience, the health and vitality of this planet will continue to worsen.

A personal commitment to helping the Earth and to reduce animal suffering, as by eating less or no meat, eggs, and dairy products, is not so much a "giving up" something in one's life as it is a giving *to* life. The personal rewards, as Les Inglis so lucidly details, are many. And, as he shows, simply eating with conscience can profoundly change one's world view or attitude toward life, as well as improve one's health. With insight, humor and feeling, the author shares his own personal transformation. This book will deeply touch and delight readers of like mind, and inspire those who do not yet feel ready to give up meat, if not also eggs and dairy products.

Above all, this is a book for all who care, if not for their own health, or for the environment, or for the animals, then at least for their children and for future generations. The world will be a better place and the future more secure when more of us can write our very own *Life After Beef*.

Dr. Michael W. Fox
Veterinarian, Humanitarian, Vegetarian
Washington, DC
September, 1991

Preface

At fifty four, I thought I had it all, had seen it all and done it all. I had fathered five sons, married three wives (sequentially), and built up a little company into a profitable public manufacturing business. I had traveled often to Europe and Asia, and I had homes in Indiana and Florida. But in a spiritual sense, I had missed one of the most important things of all — I hadn't become a vegetarian.

The morning of the day I gave up meat and other animal foods I awoke a confirmed meat eater, harboring no thought or desire to be a vegetarian. When it happened it was like a born again experience, an awakening. My sudden conversion was as much a surprise to me as it was to my friends and family. Only my wife Charlene understood my conversion because she is not only my partner in life, she was my partner in that instantaneous, discontinuous, irreversible beginning of a new way to eat, think, and live.

This is a book of telling, not selling the vegetarian experience. Much is memories of the roots of my life and their relevance to my present vegetarian lifestyle. I have tried to omit statistics and teaching about not eating animals because that task has already been done so much better than I could do it by John Robbins, Frances Moore Lappe, and Michael Klaper. While I often touch on health, I have only related my experiences and those of my family. I was trained as an engineer, not a doctor. I've tried to make this a book of feelings, reflections, and experiences, not a missionary work.

You won't find recipes for vegetarian dishes here either. Charlene's exceptional talent in the kitchen has kept my body and soul together before and after our change, eliminating the need for me to try my hand.

If you're not already a vegetarian, I hope what I have written will give you some idea of what that kind of life is like. If you are a vegetarian, I hope the book will provide a sharing experience — a chance for anyone who has given up meat to peer into the life of another on the same path. For all readers, I hope I demonstrate that being a vegetarian is not just about what one eats, it's about how one thinks and lives.

Les Inglis
Casey Key
Nokomis, Florida

SECTION 1

GETTING STARTED

It Started This Way

In the summer of 1988, Charlene and I drove to Washington DC to attend the conference of the National Alliance for Animals. We expected it to be a new experience, being the first such conference we ever attended. We didn't have any idea we were about to undergo a permanent change in our lifestyle. In fact, I'm sure if anyone had told me the conference would turn me into a vegetarian, I would have laughed out loud. If I had even thought I would be exposed to a lot of vegetarian promotion, I wouldn't have gone.

Driving through the rolling Ohio countryside and later through the much more rugged Pennsylvania part of Appalachia, we were talking and thinking about our work in the animal rights field, not our diet. We kept an eye out for antique stores, a vice we don't seem to be able to control. Darkness overtook us in Hagerstown, Maryland, and we found a hotel for the night. It wasn't much of a hotel, offering no restaurant, but the desk clerk directed us to a German restaurant close by, and we enjoyed a well prepared order of sauerbraten with red cabbage.

The next day the conference started at Georgetown University about 6 P.M. with a cocktail gathering. I thought it strange there was no cheese among the hors d'oeuvres, but I put it out of my mind and made do with the fruits and vegetables — after all we were going out to dinner later.

An informal session followed the reception. The attendees were asked for a show of hands to determine how many ate meat or fish and how many practiced one or another form of vegetarianism. I was astounded at how many in the audience ate no meat, fish, dairy products, or eggs. Those strict vegetarians called themselves "vegans," a new word for me. We broke up into small groups headed by the conference lecturers, and mine was headed by Dr. Michael Klaper, a very lean and healthy looking man who is the director of EarthSave Foundation and a proponent of vegan nutrition. Others in our group included the siblings of actor River Phoenix — all vegans.

Dr. Klaper invited us to share any thoughts about animals with our small group, and I, having already heard more about vegetarians than animals, said something like, "I don't think you have to be a vegetarian to work for and care about animals, nor do you have to care about animals to be a vegetarian." Today I'd have to eat those words.

The meeting broke up, and we went to a little Italian restaurant in Georgetown remembered from a previous trip. I put away a beautifully prepared portion of calamari without once thinking about the living ocean squid it had been. Washington is a wonderful place for a meat eater with a taste for the unusual.

By breakfast the next morning, I was worried the conference was going to be just as much about vegetarianism as about animals. I was uncomfortable and defensive. Charlene didn't seem to mind as much as I did. As we passed through the Marriott buffet, I loaded up with pancakes, link sausages, and scrambled eggs, telling Charlene I didn't think I was ready for an entire weekend of vegetarian propaganda. Summoning bravado to hide my fears, I forked a blackened link sausage, waved it around, and said, "Wait till I tell those skinny vegetarian guys about the he-man breakfast I'm having this morning."

To tell the truth, at 6'3" and 200 pounds, I needed to lose some weight, too much of which could be seen around my neck and waist. Unfortunately I never had been able to push myself away from all those wonderful dishes I could pick off menus, dooming myself to live in the middle of some unsightly rings of fat.

On Saturday the conference terminated my life as a meat eater. In addition to lots about animals, during the day we had lectures by Dr. Klaper, John Robbins, the author of *Diet for a New America,* and Dr. Neal Barnard, the articulate leader of the Physicians Committee for Responsible Medicine. These three vegans are undoubtedly the most well informed and convincing men on the subject of not eating animals in the world. My defensive, emotional efforts to protect my gourmand status gave way to attention; attention gave way to belief; and belief gave way to a new conviction. They were so skillful, their message so compelling, so sincerely presented, it could not be denied.

Lunch was a vegan meal at a Gerogetown University dining room, and as we prepared to go out to dinner, I said to Charlene, "You know, there must be something to this vegetarian stuff after all." She, of course, had heard the same lectures, and she was even more ready to make the change than I was. We ate meatless pasta that night, never again returning to meat, fish, dairy products, or eggs.

We finished the conference with a new appreciation of our work for the animals. We knew we were helping them in another important way now, while doing good things for our own health. We bought *Diet for a New America* at the conference and had John Robbins autograph it for us. Today it is our most used reference book. We both feel better these days. My cholesterol went from 296 to the low 160's, and more than 20 pounds of spare tire type weight has left my body without any conscious effort to limit the amount I eat. I know neither of us will ever go back to our old lifestyle.

Our vegetarian life is easier because we are doing it together. Trying new dishes, finding new foods, seeking out restaurants to serve us vegan food are challenges, but also a new common ground between us. It takes lots of label reading, experimentation in the kitchen, and toleration of a number of mediocre meals until the right tricks are learned. You work through awkward moments when invited out. All in all becoming a vegetarian is easy and pleasant — and it does wonderful things for your health and the suffering animals.

SECTION TWO

GOING WAY BACK

When We Were Kids

I can't be certain where or when the seeds of thought finally resulting in my becoming a vegetarian were planted in my head. Robbins, Klaper, and Barnard, who talked us into the big change, must have been talking to minds prepared to make the switch, even if my mind did not consciously know it was prepared. I wasn't thinking about becoming a vegetarian — far from it — that day I was particularly defensive on the subject, not wanting to change what I ate. What made me susceptible to the vegetarian message?

The best I can do is guess it all stemmed from early attitudes about health and animals instilled in me by my parents. Our small family included myself, my sister Jean, and my parents, and I don't think we were unusual in any way. We lived in pleasant city areas and later in the suburbs; we had a stable, not affluent life; Dad worked and Mom stayed at home; and my sister and I were expected to do our homework, follow the rules, and occasionally help out like doing dishes and mowing the lawn.

On health matters, Mom and Dad had the attitudes of normal, intelligent people. Mom told us how little all the trappings of life would mean if we did not have our health. I'm sure she never thought about being a vegetarian in her entire life — at least until I became one — but you could tell from the way she cooked and cleaned house she knew lots about nutrition (in the conventional sense) and sanitation. Jean and I were popped into the tub for baths at the slightest provocation. I remember one day when I was ten my outdoor activities earned me three baths as I kept getting into messes — probably an all time record for me. Those baths were at Mom's insistence, not on my own initiative.

Mom's feelings about health were behind many of our trials as children including regular trips to the doctor and dentist, immunizations, and vaccinations.

At about six or seven, Jean came down with scarlet fever. In those days someone from the city health department came out and nailed a sign up on your front door, and I was ecstatic to learn I would miss the next few weeks of school when I wasn't even sick. What seemed at first like a great stroke of luck quickly became a scourge as I realized I couldn't play outside or see my friends. I even had to stay out of Jean's room. During those weeks our house was a steamy prison for me as Mom sterilized everything repeatedly. Her diligent nursing and sanitizing must have paid off because Jean's case was mild, leaving no after-effects, and I didn't get scarlet fever.

Dad supported Mom in her wars on dirt and germs. Together they led healthy lives rarely being taken sick and never seriously so. Neither of them had ever smoked, but they talked about smoking often. Jean and I grew up adamant we would never be smokers thanks to constant brainwashing from our parents. We knew smoking was dangerous, causing fires, and unhealthy, causing cancer and other problems. Besides it was messy, annoying to others, and expensive. Later when we both took up smoking as young adults, I'm sure Mom and Dad felt pains we didn't know about at the time. Neither of us, however, were ever able to smoke without guilt, and we each eventually quit with the help, I'm sure, of the antismoking ethic we inherited from Mom and Dad.

My attitudes about health have haunted me most of my adult life. I couldn't smoke without guilt, somehow knowing I was slowly killing myself. In a similar way, for a long time before becoming a vegetarian, I wondered and worried about fats, cholesterol, the amount of food I ate, whether I was getting enough exercise, etc. I probably didn't live much differently from most people, but I worried more — thanks to the extra sensitivity on health burned into my brain by Mom and Dad.

If I found an article in the newspaper about health, I usually read it giving more food for thought to my worrying system. About five years ago I ran across an article about how heart disease can be predicted by observing the earlobes. It said those with a propensity for heart disease will display a diagonal crease across the earlobe, while those who don't have the crease are less likely to have heart problems. My worrying system drove me up out of my chair and into the bathroom to regard my earlobes in the mirror. Terror gripped me as I stared at the awful truth—a clearly developed crease cut across each earlobe! By this time, my Dad had long since passed away, dying unexpectedly and suddenly from his first heart attack, and I was well aware that certain heart problems are passed on by heredity. That article ruined my whole day and several others as well.

Dad's death at 67 years old had been a worry to me. That seemed so young. My big hope was I had inherited longevity from my mother's side where several relatives had lived into their 90's. I took the bad news about my ear lobes to Mom, who was then in her mid 80's. Mom smiled as she told me, "I heard about that idea many years ago when I was young. If you look at my earlobes, you'll see I have the crease too." Mom dismissed the earlobe theory as an old wives' tale, and I stopped worrying about my own earlobes. I still think about some reporter passing that stuff off as news when Mom had heard it as a girl.

✠✠✠

My attitudes about animals also grew out of my early family life. I started out really afraid of dogs. At age three or four walking to and from the stores with Mom passing a house where a dog barked at us, I was terrified. I made my feelings clear to Mom whenever we passed that house. At that time we lived only two blocks from a pleasant square surrounded by shops, and Mom shopped for food and household items several times a week. She wheeled Jean in a stroller, guided me on a harness and leash, and carried a bag of groceries home with her. She didn't need the problem of a screaming three-year old, tethered on a leash, trying to run the other way whenever that dog decided to bark. Mom and Dad solved the problem by getting Jean and me a Cocker Spaniel.

Chessie was beyond the puppy stage when he came to our house, but he was still the neatest thing that had ever happened to us. Twenty five pounds of honey blond silk followed by a thumbsized stub signalling happiness by twitching side to side. This was heaven. We learned about sniffs and licks and romps and even snaps when we pestered him too much. To us, they had found the perfect gift, a new member of the family far more welcome than another brother or sister would have been. To Mom and Dad, Chessie was loved and respected, but I know Mom would have preferred to live without pets. For them and for me, Chessie was a cure to my unreasoning fear of dogs and the beginning of a lifelong love of animals, especially of the canine types.

Dad was quick to teach us that dogs had feelings too. Chessie had come from a family with no children, expecting a bit more space than we kids allowed him. Patiently and often, Dad showed us how to enjoy Chessie while considering his feelings. Soon he was accompanying us on Mom's trips to the stores. Eventually busy traffic took its toll on one of the shopping trips sadly ending Chessie's life, but not before we had learned to respect animals as fellow beings with feelings and needs. We all—Dad and Mom included — cried for a long time when he died. Several years passed and we moved to the suburbs before we got another dog.

I don't think Dad had many pets when he was young, and I'm not sure where his empathic feelings about animals came from, but they were there on display for Jean and me to follow. Mom had been raised on a farm, so animals were not strangers to her. She had a more utilitarian view of them than Dad did as you might expect, but she had respect and consideration too. Our dogs got the same good care we kids received, and I know they got baths more often than anyone else's. I suspect Mom's penchant for cleanliness was one reason she preferred to live without pets. In spite of it she got us our pets when we needed then.

As we grew up we were often exposed to animals in ways appropriate to the little city slickers we were. We tripped to the zoo, took pony rides, watched Grandma's chickens and Grandpa's bees. Later, in the suburbs, pheasants lived in the fields near home. Dad never hunted in his life, but some of our neighbors would tramp through those fields after the pheasants. By then Dad's ethic had transferred to me, and I could see no sport in killing those birds.

Attitudes about animals and health are at the root of my choice to be a vegetarian. As I become more informed and committed to vegetarian life, I feel I am but building on a foundation prepared for me by two people, both now departed, neither vegetarians, who loved me and carefully impressed their ethical values on me.

Just Like Mom Used to Make

Raised on a Missouri farm in the early years of this century, Mom learned to cook from her mother, another talented lady in the kitchen. As anyone who has ever lived on a farm will tell you, the life is mostly hard work, but it has its special moments like evenings on the porch swing, a "never too busy to stop and visit" ethic, and, perhaps most memorable, those meals! Hearty enough to fuel the biggest farm hand, varied to tempt any taste with several vegetables, potatoes, breads, jams and jellies, and more. That's the way it was on most farms, and that's the way it was at Grandma's house.

Grandma held forth in a huge kitchen, undoubtedly sized based on its relative importance to all the other functions of the house. A giant wood stove commanded the focal point of the room, so big and so heavy I thought the house had been built around it. Hatches for fire tending and little ovens and a cubby for firewood took up the sides, and squat Queen Anne feet held it off a floor covered with an asbestos pad. The top was full of circular holes, each covered with a cast iron plate. The plate for the largest hole was a series of concentric rings, each with a socket for the handle used to remove them. That handle and the handles on the oven doors were shiny wonders encircled with shaped wire springs to keep your hand from touching the hot part. Above and to the rear of the cooking surface a warming shelf spanned the entire width of the stove, bisected by the stovepipe.

A sturdy old worktable stood in the center of the big room. Grandma sometimes used it for eating a quick meal, but most often for rolling dough, assembling pies, and staging dishes about to be cooked or just completed. The sink didn't have running water, but if you went out on the porch and pumped the handle up and down, water would run.

Two newer stoves completed the kitchen equipment. These were in white porcelain, one fueled with coal oil and one with propane gas. They had large ovens, more like Mom's modern stove back home in the city. Grandma seemed to prefer these stoves in the order of their age with the oldest, the wood stove, being used every day and most often. The others weren't neglected, especially on Sundays when the entire clan including all her grandchildren, my cousins, converged for a farm style family dinner. She cooked so much food, so many different dishes, that every stove was at full temperature filling the kitchen with steam and smoke and smells of chicken frying, biscuits baking, vegetable soup simmering.

Most of us think back to our Grandmothers as kindly, comfortable old ladies who smiled at us a lot and loved us — my Grandma was no exception—but at times like those Sundays when there were so many people around waiting to eat that she organized sequential sittings at the big old dining room table, it was best not to get in her way. Aided by Mom and my aunts, the farm kitchen became a no-nonsense factory turning out a product we all wanted — Sunday dinner. Heaven help the kid who got in their way in there. Smiles and loves were best sought at other times.

The meals Grandma cooked were some of the most memorable in my childhood. The table seemed to sag a little as dish after dish was set out for us. Except for the meat course, Grandma's style was to provide at least two different dishes for each part of the meal. Biscuits showed up with freshly baked bread to join the covered compotes of preserves on the table all the time, and each meal featured a creamed vegetable and at least one other simply boiled. Creamed peas were my favorite of all her vegetables. Only one meat dish was served — almost always chicken, either roasted or fried. I can't remember ever once having beef at Grandma's house, and except for bacon, other red meats were a rarity. This reflected the economy of a small family farm in Missouri from the time before my childhood. They raised plant foods, and except for a yard full of chickens, didn't farm meat. Grandpa's products were the biggest tomatoes I've ever seen — Big Boys and Winsalls—plus corn, beans, and peas and apples, plums, and cherries from the orchard.

By the time I came into the family and began to visit them, there were no farm animals at my grandparents' home except the chickens and bees. They had lost their 80 acres in the depression and had moved to an old farmhouse at the edge of Paris, Missouri, their lifelong community, where Grandpa still had the biggest and best vegetable garden in those parts. In Mom's childhood there would have been a cow kept for milk, horses or a donkey for the plow (thought of as pets by Mom and her two brothers), and rarely a pig. Grandpa gave up on pigs after slaughter times produced more grief from the kids who loved them than their meat produced in pleasurable eating. In reality, their farm was more nearly vegetarian than the typical household of today.

This then was the classroom where Mom learned to cook. Like most kids, I thought Mom and Grandma were the greatest cooks in the world. Years later after separation from a failed first marriage, I lived alone for a while and wished I could cook like Mom. Even then she helped with hints and tips. Her cooking had changed from Grandma's because she had raised her family in the city. She had running water, electric refrigeration, well stocked food stores, and later supermarkets. Mom cooked things I imagine Grandma seldom tasted and almost never prepared like lamb and ocean fish and lots of beef. As she tried to help me learn to cook, she certainly wasn't making a vegetarian out of me.

Paris, Missouri, where Grandma lived and Mom learned, was also the home town of a well known cookbook author of an earlier day, Mary Margaret McBride. Having produced no one else who gained national recognition, Paris people all talked about Mary Margaret, and even a visiting grandkid like me soon came to know about her. Later as an adult I had separated and was living alone trying to learn how to cook. Happily I discovered Mary Margaret McBride's cookbook had been serialized and was offered at the local supermarket in installments shipped weekly complete with a screw post binder cover for the dozen sections. Even more happily, the offering had been available for some time so I didn't have to keep coming back as each section arrived at the store; they were all there already in the display. I picked up twelve sections and the binder and practically skipped home with a four inch thick, full page sized book complete with pictures and many hundreds of pages — all devoted to cooking *just like Grandma used to do.*

By this time Grandma was long gone and Mom lived in Florida while I lived in Ohio. Mom's contributions to my cooking education were limited to advice given on my occasional visits with her. The McBride book, however, was a bridge to my own past — to family dinners on summer trips to Missouri and to steaming bowls of creamed peas and plates of fried chicken and cooked onions and mushrooms. How could one guy get so lucky? I still have the book stuck way up on a shelf and seldom opened now that I'm married to Mom's successor as the world's greatest cook and personally retired from the culinary arts.

In the last two and one half years of her life, Mom witnessed incredulously my sudden and total change to vegetarian life. She saw Charlene and me going at vegetarian eating with great gusto, relishing the challenges of finding new ethnic foods, learning to cook them, finding suitable restaurants, cooking for guests, etc. I'm sure she thought our giving up meat was probably the result of Charlene's intense interest in the rights of animals and that I had been dragged into becoming vegetarian. But she was wrong — I was as committed as Charlene. When Mom, after further discussion understood that to us vegetarian meant no chicken, no fish, and (heaven help us) no eggs or dairy products, I know she thought we were both crazy. Still she was a good sport about it.

You'd have to be a good sport to watch your only son turn away from all those "good" foods he had been eating his whole life. What had happened to the years of loving meals she had prepared masterfully demonstrating the joys of every kind of animal food? Were all of her efforts, not to mention her mother's efforts, to establish me in a life of rich culinary variety now to be thrown away by a couple of otherwise seemingly intelligent kids chanting about health, animal suffering, and the environment — thrown away in favor of green beans, peas, and potatoes? Oh the shame of it all.

Fortunately, by the time we converted, Mom didn't do much cooking for others anymore. She still cooked for herself and made interesting (if nonveg) meals. We preferred to take her out to eat on our visits to Florida, so we wouldn't add to her workload and so we could sample the many restaurants near where she lived. Also we had a second home near her, so Charlene often had her come to our house to dinner, and she always enjoyed Charlene's vegetarian cooking. The good sport in Mom showed through when she did have us to dinner a very few times. While her vegetarian meals were not as imaginative or as practiced as those we had at home, she cooked good food we were happy to eat. I would have expected no less than her heartfelt efforts to please us, and I will remember those times as long as I live.

Our culinary style was an enigma to Mom as she listened to my talk about cholesterol and Charlene's talk about animals suffering in factory farms. She was always polite, but behind those loving hazel eyes she had to be thinking, "What a waste." We, on the other hand, were thinking, "What a wonderful way to live."

Dad, Meateater Extrordinaire

Far from being a vegetarian, Dad was a champion meateater. He saw nothing wrong with it, living in a time when the effects of animal fats on one's health were not well understood. I remember as a young boy asking about the meat we were eating. "Dad, isn't this really a dead animal?" I asked, not as a challenge but as a point of information. "No son, this is cooked beef," he replied, sincerely believing he had made a distinction worth noting. In my trust I accepted his distinction and was never really bothered by the real nature of meat again until I became a vegetarian.

When we moved to the suburbs, Dad bought the largest size Weber grill he could find. He built a table for it, equipped himself with barbecue tools, and began a long career as griller of steaks and cooker of meats. It wasn't long after World War II and Americans had just emerged from a long period of shortages and rationing of meat. Moving to the suburbs, grilling steaks outside in your backyard, and no longer having to worry about quotas, ration books, and shortages was the new "good life" Americans developed for themselves, and Dad was right there to insure his little brood gorged themselves in it.

Barbecuing, then and now, is not just a means of preparing a meal. It is also an opportunity to acquire an array of toys and to play with them, all in the name of the serious business of cooking food. For Dad, the toys included, in addition to the grill, a set of barbecue tools with wooden handles and leather thongs, a cypress table he built with sprawling work areas on either side of the grill and sprouting hooks for storing the tools, an assortment of barbecue sauces and the pastry brushes to apply them, and man-sized shakers of salt, pepper, and seasoned salt.

Cooking out was announced to and received by the family with all the happy anticipation of going to a movie or a carnival. In the first act, Dad appeared in chef's hat and apron and began the ritual of starting the charcoal — a craft even unto itself. He opened the vents on the Weber to settings he had scientifically determined would promote ignition of the charcoal rapidly and uniformly. Utensils, flavoring, serving dishes, and a squirt bottle of water to control flames were all arranged on the barbecue table like a surgeon's tools prepared for an appendectomy. Mom, a dedicated stagehand, worked offstage in the kitchen wrapping potatoes in foil, soaking corn in its husks,and chopping up a salad. A top billing performer in her own right, Mom never stepped out of her supporting role when Dad was cooking out.

The second act was the cooking itself. Dad spread white coals evenly across the grating, added soaked hickory chips to the charcoal, further fine tuned the Weber vents, and scraped the grill surface now sterilized by the heat. Wrapped potatoes were placed at the edges of the coals on the grate; the grill was replaced; and half its surface was covered with corn. After a short wait to give the vegetables a head start, Dad speared the steak with his big fork, lifted it from the platter, and dropped it onto the grill as it was enveloped in a cloud of steam and smoke. The entire assemblage was quickly snuffed with the cover of the grill. Now the smoke mixed with steam blew forcefully out the top vents and Dad began a program of lifting the cover to turn, apply sauces, turn again, poke, and take test cuts. All the while he delivered a running commentary on the process, a speech made increasingly more fluent by the gradual consumption of a few glasses of wine.

Act three was the dramatic crescendo, and all of us became bit players as our plates were loaded with food and we repaired to our usual places at the big round picnic table Dad had made from the bottom of a cypress washing vat. At nine feet in diameter, it was so big, he had to equip it with a lazy susan for passing around the various side dishes and seasonings. We all dug in.

We talked about everything at mealtimes, including the food we were eating. One Sunday, Dad had just read a new theory on weight control when he recapped it for us: "Eat the fat and stay lean," we were told. Apparently, someone had written an article actually suggesting that if you didn't trim off the marginal fat from meats and ate it along with the leaner parts, you would be less likely to gain weight. That idea, however difficult to accept, satisfied Dad, and he stopped cutting the fat of the edges off the steaks. It's a wonder we didn't all have weight problems, but Jean and I were skinny kids, Mom was a normal size, and Dad didn't have too much weight until his later years, and even then it never looked too bad on his tall frame.

Except for occasional visits back home, Jean's and my participation in Dad's barbecues stopped in the mid 1950's when she married a Navy man and I married and entered the Air Force right after college. Now it's all memories of Dad producing and directing his barbecuing extravaganzas designed to appeal to every sense of his family and guests. I'm staggered to think he and Mom ever begat a child who became a vegetarian.

SECTION THREE

VEGETARIAN LIFE

Talking a Good Vegetarian Game

My vegetarian lifestyle is a part of every moment of my existence. I am as comfortable with it as I am with a well worn pair of flannel pajamas on a cold night. And while I'm aware that most of the rest of society has at least subconscious reservations about vegetarians, thinking of us as dietary deviates, I'm nevertheless quick to tell a new acquaintance about what I eat, and I'm always amazed at how often I hear in response to my disclosure, "Oh yes, I'm almost a vegetarian these days, myself," or, "I know, I hardly eat any red meat anymore."

If the number of people who readily claim to be nearly vegetarian really were so, half the fast food restaurants in this country would be featuring tofu and seitan. Just as it's more common to talk a good game of baseball than it is to play it, so it is with eating as a vegetarian.

For the most part Americans are quite well informed about health. I rush to add that being informed and internalizing and acting on that knowledge are entirely different matters. For example, consider cigarette smoking, now so broadly considered a serious health hazard that you would be hard-pressed to find a person (other than someone in the tobacco industry) denying the dangers of smoking. And such a rare individual would be considered truly ignorant by the rest of us. Despite general agreement on the harmful effects, millions of people — a significant percentage of the population — still smoke.

It wasn't always so with smoking. I can remember doctors in cigarette ads, and doctors who smoked were much more numerous than today. And although the slang phrases, "coffin nails" and "cancer sticks," were applied to cigarettes before I was born, forty or fifty years ago cigarettes were not generally believed to be harmful. Only study after study, a rising incidence of lung and heart problems, and a succession of attorneys general pointing their fingers at tobacco over many years has brought about today's conventional wisdom on the subject.

Our use of tobacco demonstrates that as a society we are quite capable of knowing about a health hazard and failing to change our lifestyles to avoid it. It isn't any different with our meat eating. How many studies have been reported in the news linking a diet high in saturated fats to heart disease, strokes, etc? In the last twenty years or so, such news has appeared so frequently that the average person has certainly conceded the connection at least on an intellectual level. Unfortunately, at the emotional level where we all live, with meat eating far more even than with smoking, it is a case of being informed, but not convinced.

And after all, the information we get on the dangers of animal fats in our diets is far from specific on what we need to do to make ourselves healthy. It is almost always qualitative — "fats, especially animal fats are bad for you" — rather than quantitative — "you should restrict yourself to so many milligrams of saturated fat per day per pound of body weight." And it never makes the statement, "The optimum amount of saturated animal fat in your diet should be____." That optimum amount could well be zero, but even those who know very well the health dangers of meat eating — people like doctors working on cholesterol disorders — are reluctant to tell you to give up meat eating entirely. Among other things, it isn't good marketing for doctors to ask their patients to make such a drastic change. It is still too easy for any patient to seek out a second opinion and find another doctor who will say just to cut down a little.

Armed with qualitative knowledge and lacking quantitative specifics, the nonveg does what I did when I was one — he fools himself into thinking he has responded adequately. He has passed up the pork chops at lunch in favor of a chef's salad hiding beneath strips of ham and cheese and about 3 $^1/_2$ ounces of Thousand Island dressing. Maybe that's less red meat, but it isn't going to help him much. Sometimes he'll choose fish thinking vegetarians eat fish, don't they? And of course he's always safe with the heart healthy choices the chef marks on the menu with little hearts in the margin. Today's chef's heart selection is $^1/_3$ pound of lean ground round, no bun, with buttered string beans and a Waldorf salad loaded with mayonnaise. Not only do we like to fool ourselves about dietary health matters, there are plenty of doctors, chefs, newspaper columnists, and even some nutritionists who are glad to help us fool ourselves.

When I tell a new nonveg friend I'm a vegetarian and he responds with a comment about his dwindling consumption of red meat, he's not telling me he agrees with me in thought, spirit, or principle; he is trying to reassure himself he is following a healthy diet. In reality, we are poles apart.

I'm afraid it will be a long time before meat eating is generally recognized to be harmful like smoking presently is. As a society, we've received enough information to tickle our consciences about the problems with animal foods, but we are offered too many ways to let us off the hook. Meat eating is a far more universally practiced habit than smoking ever was. With the exception of a few lucky kids born to committed vegetarian parents, each of us takes up meat eating as soon as the first jars of baby food are pried open to supplement the formula or mother's milk we started with.

Stronger influences than the meat tastes in the baby food are the family activities around us when we are small. If Mom cooks lots of meat, eggs, and dairy products, certainly we are going to eat them. What alternatives do small children have? Older brothers and sisters are great examples for our monkey-like mimicry. If they bend our twig by showing us their love for burgers, ice cream, and sausage pizza, that's the way our tree will grow.

A nonveg society will tend to stay that way until something happens to convince most people that another way of eating is better. In general, people today are far from convinced, and until they are, they will act to protect and perpetuate their nonveg feeding.

Advertising Our Philosophy

Only in the last two or three decades have tee shirts been used to project one's philosophical views to others. Now few clubs or organizations fail to create their own tee shirts with slogans, philosophy, wisdom, or even attacks on others. Printing specialized messages and graphics on tee shirts is a huge business, fed by our individual desires to tell others something about ourselves and feeding our widely practiced covert reading of everyone else's shirt. You can learn a little about someone else without even meeting that person merely by reading his shirt. If you sense a kindred spirit, the tee shirt message is an ideal way to open a conversation. Conversely, a tee shirt displaying an alien philosophy performs a valuable service both for you and its owner when you are warned away.

Bumper stickers have some of the same functions as tee shirts, but they are slightly less personal and do little to facilitate meetings of kindred spirits, unless they say, "honk if you're horny." They have the disadvantage of sometimes inviting rude or aggressive behavior in traffic from drivers strongly opposed to the views put forth by your bumper sticker. Recently Charlene and I were in the midst of a traffic jam in Chattanooga, Tennessee as two interstate routes wrestled their way into one. The pattern had settled down into a reasonably civil alternation of one from I24 and then one from I75, and most drivers patiently waited their turns. When our turn came, a pickup truck jacked up high over its wheels pushed its way in front of us ahead of its turn. Our choice was fall back or bend fenders, so we yielded wondering why this driver had risked an accident to break a pattern working so well. Once in front of us we saw his National Rifle Association sticker and an "I support bowhunting" sticker. He had been reacting to Charlene's GO VEGAN Florida license plate, her license plate frame stating, "Animals have rights too," and her bumper sticker proclaiming, "Fur is dead." Few are the hunters today who don't impute to such a display an active anti-hunting philosophy. This one, upset or threatened by our advertised beliefs, had acted out his little revenge.

Balancing that negative encounter I recall an earlier simulated Indiana license plate she had shouting "WEAR NO FUR" from the front of her car. At a shopping center I drove into a parking place while two ladies turned around and applauded to show their similar beliefs. We've learned to expect approval and disapproval on occasion, but I think the real value of tee shirts, bumper stickers, pins, hats, license plates, etc. is in their effect on those who show us no reaction at all.

Major advertisers know countless brief exposures to their messages cause people to try their products. Some even use repetitive annoying commercials to brand their messages onto our brains (remember "What do doctors do?"). Politicians put their name on every lamppost and in every front yard at election time. Every day thousands of messages assault us trying to shape our attitudes or prompt us to some action.

If you're selling soap or cars or any big consumer item, you can afford television and radio spots, billboards, magazines, and newspaper ads. If you're a member of a small club or an individual grassroots activist for any cause, tee shirts and bumper stickers will fit your budget. Regardless of the medium, repeated exposure gets the message across.

The vegetarian tee shirts in my closet offer a variety of messages. "Pigs are my friends, not my food," says one. Another works the vegetarian message in with an animal rights theme saying, "Animals are not ours to eat, wear, or experiment on." One modestly states, "Be kind to animals, don't eat them." Our Cincinnati Vegetarian Society shirts proclaim growth with, "Vegetarians are sprouting up all over."

Thousands of passers-by are compelled to read these messages about eating meat or not. Every little exposure to an idea is like a drop of water running down a mountain — by itself, inconsequential, but when combined with all the other exposures, capable of wearing down the mountain. I wear my tee shirts because I think each time I do, it helps to promote acceptability and understanding of the lifestyle. Who knows, perhaps someday far in the future restaurants, in addition to having smoking and nonsmoking sections in the dining room, will have vegetarian and nonvegetarian sections on the menu.

The Restaurant Blues

Going out to eat has been one of the pleasures of my entire life. After college it was a rare treat, my slim budget allowing little extra for such fun, but gradually, as the years passed, budgetary constraints governed bigger expenditures and restauranting was hardly inhibited. As a nonveg, the supply and variety of restaurants seemed endless, and I would readily write one off for poor service or bad cooking, smug in the knowledge so many were still left that each time we decided to eat out, we faced the dilemma of selecting only one from the many possibilities. How different is our restauranting today as total vegetarians.

As a result of my vegetarian persuasion, I now define a good restaurant as one which has something — some one thing — I can eat. No longer do I demand an entire list of possibilities to ponder and pick over. Instead I'm delighted if I can find one totally vegetarian dish like ratatouille or stir fried vegetables on a menu.

In my nonveg days, I hated ordering special things, knowing it was like throwing dice with the waiter's tenuous command of English and a busy chef's questionable disposition in a hot kitchen. I picked from the menu, asked for no variations, and expected the establishment at least to be able to do a good job preparing a meal they had designed themselves. Today, nearly everything I order in a restaurant is special in some way. In a more perfect world, it wouldn't be this way.

The main problem with restaurants is most of them don't understand what a vegetarian is. How many waitresses have said, in response to my disclosure I am a vegetarian, "No problem, we have some nice seafood dishes."? How often has a vegetable dish arrived in a cream sauce I can't eat or a tossed salad been set before me with a wedge of hard boiled egg smiling up at me from the bowl? Are so few of us vegetarians around that restaurant people should have no idea which foods we can and cannot eat?

When Charlene and I came back home from Washington in 1988 after our conversion, we stayed overnight in a Holiday Inn in Cambridge, Ohio — not exactly a sophisticated place to look for our first vegetarian meal on the road. As beginners, we avoided the chain fast food places on the highway and elected to eat at the hotel. As I opened the menu, my heart sank — this chef was a real meat and potatoes kind of guy. You could have anything you want if the main part of it was beef, pork, fish, or chicken, and no part of it involved green vegetables. We finally got them to fetch up a halfway decent dinner of baked potatoes, cooked onions, and apple pie. We were only beginning to learn the art of quizzing a waitress who acted like she had never met a vegetarian before as we sorted down through their limited resources and abilities and cajoled them into presenting something we could eat.

In the always challenging, seldom completely satisfying restaurant game we now play as vegetarians, one of my pet peeves is to get through well to a waitress only to have the chef screw the meal up to a fare-thee-well. Our local Friday's restaurant offered a variety of dishes which, with minor modifications, could be acceptable. One night I had selected a pasta and vegetable dish served as a casserole which really sounded good. I ascertained from the waitress it could be prepared without the cheese mentioned in the menu, and watched as she wrote "no cheese" on the order. When our food came, of course my dinner had cheese melted over the top. "No problem, I'll get them to do it right in just a minute," she said leaving Charlene her dinner and me with nothing. Sure enough, in a few minutes she was back with one without cheese. Now famished from watching my wife eat and smelling her food, I tore into mine like Roscoe, our dog, attacks his food. A couple of minutes later I was wondering what's this sticky mess binding up on my fork, and then I knew what happened.

Of course the mess of was cheese. The cook's solution had been to strip away the cheese melted on top of the dish rather than make another one without cheese — the cheese that had melted into the interior of the casserole was still there. Not concealing my disgust, I gave the waitress back the sticky mess and refused to order anything else; I was too upset, Charlene was too far along, and we wanted to make it to the movie in time. The Friday's manager, a nice young lady, came over apologizing profusely. She agreed the cook should never have taken the short cut and told us our dinner was on the house. I know that cook got trained, but I wouldn't bet the ranch the one there today knows any better.

The same thing has happened to us with anchovies being removed by hand from putanesca, bits of pork being separated from Chinese dishes, etc. We always try to be sure we won't get food prepared ahead of time and then doctored to our requirements, but, try as we will, we don't always get through. When we reach a point of frustration sufficient to remove one more establishment from our personal approved list we feel a big loss, perhaps bigger than the restaurant feels. There just aren't that many possibilities around anymore.

✖✖✖

The first pizza I ever had was as a freshman at Northwestern. At that time there wasn't any pizzeria in the small town in the Chicago suburbs where I grew up. A fraternity brother had been down to Howard Street drinking beer with some of the boys (Howard Street was the last street in Chicago before you got to Evanston, home to both Northwestern and the Women's Christian Temperance Union). They had ordered up a couple of large pizzas and brought what they couldn't eat back to the fraternity house. It was after dinner and my hollow leg made me the only taker when the pizza was offered to us lizards draped around the TV lounge. Ordering extra cheese and double anchovies would get you about the same thing in a pizzeria today, but then it was just an anchovy pizza, and I thought it was the best thing I had ever tasted.

Not long after we took up the ways of the vegetarian, my pizza thermostat called for some energy, and I began to think here's one more thing I'll have to do without from now on, but then it occurred to me it ought to be possible to construct a pizza to the rigid standards of a total vegetarian. Countless other vegs must have worked out the pizza puzzle before me, but I had none of them around for advice, and my body was underdosed on pizza and complaining about it. We talked over the possibilities and headed up the road from our country retreat to the nearest pizzeria fourteen miles away in a town of 2000 people. There were plenty of vegetable toppings, and three of my favorites were onions, peppers, and olives. The big gamble was to try it without cheese, but the gamble paid off — we had a great meal, and my body slipped into satisfied inactivity something like a python that has just swallowed a rabbit.

When we ordered our veg pizza, the teenagers behind the counter did a double take that would make a vaudevillian proud. Cooking it was easy for them, but once it was in the oven, they had their heads together at the counter, pencils scratching at notepads, while they kept looking back at the prices in the menu. Finally, when the pizza was ready, we were presented with a bill for the best bargain we've ever had when buying pizza. The head scratching, number crunching session, they explained, had been to decide how much to deduct for the cheese. These young folks had reasoned out that cheese was one of the more expensive components of any pizza and that if you charged for extra cheese, you should deduct for no cheese, so that's what they did. Unfortunately, every other pizzeria we have visited since then is happy to charge us for the extras, but never makes a subtraction for deleting cheese.

✠✠✠

Lord save me from trendy restaurants thrown up (?) all over the country in great chains with pop culture menus and nubile servers with name tags, smiling and reciting their lines. I haven't found one yet a veg can really be proud of. In Florida, there's one near our house that arrived seemingly overnight, a windowless clapboard box with a wheelchair ramp and their trendy sign painted in florescent colors glowing in the night. Now I know every one of these new age greasy spoons has to come up with supposedly unique ways to dish up their animal fats, but I had never reflected on the pains they take to find cute new attention getting names and slogans until this one came along. This one proudly proclaimed to the world out front they serve "warm beer and lousy food." The short end to this story is to say I was warned. The longer end I'm compelled to record is the story of when we went in to see if they had a few items a vegetarian could eat.

We specified non-smoking and were shown to a table along the wall in the middle of a long room. That's progress, I thought, because Florida is the most backwards of the populous states in establishing non smoking area in restaurants. Most menu items were fish, in keeping with their waterfront location, but we did find a salad and deep fried mushrooms in the list of appetizers. Making do, as I often must, that's what I had, and I'm still sorry I bothered. A passable salad came out first, and it seemed to take forever to get the mushrooms. When they finally arrived, their thick breaded coatings were so completely grease soaked, they were soft. They had been cooked crisp, but not drained, and now merely molesting them with a fork caused the coating to fall away and the slippery, glistening mushroom inside to be exposed. It was a blessing because no one, veg or nonveg, should ingest the glop they called breading.

A large table next to us with about eight people around it lit up their cigarettes, and the smoke wafted our way. Charlene, who is particularly sensitive to smoke, signalled the waitress and asked if we had really been placed in the non-smoking area, indicating the ceremonial fires at the next table. "You are in the non-smoking area, ma'am; it ends right here," she smiled as her arm drew an imaginary line across the restaurant neatly bisecting the two feet between her chair and one at the smoking table. Our smoky wait for the check was exceeded only by the wait for the mushrooms, and we were finally sprung to the free world and fresh air outside, faithfully promising the little parole officers in our minds we would never darken their doormat again. Some slogan. It should have read, "warm beer, lousy food, bad service, and a rotten menu."

⌖⌖⌖

Chinese restaurants offer their own inscrutable challenges to a vegetarian. Cheese and other dairy products are not an issue, and eggs are easy to identify and avoid, but you can still be fouled up by a chinese menu. As a rule, the menu is listed under headings like chicken, pork, beef, and (happily) vegetables. Under vegetables you may find broccoli, string beans, mixed vegetables, mushrooms and tofu (apparently written, "bean curd," in some Chinese dialects) all served on soft noodles, crisp noodles, or rice. Pretty good as far as it goes, but you still have to be careful and ask questions.

The Chinese have a tradition of using bits of meat as condiments or flavoring in their food. Nearly every Chinese menu I've seen heads the vegetable section with the word "vegetables," not with the word "vegetarian." They mean vegetables are the primary component of the dish; they are not necessarily promising no meat. I've learned you have to ask. (In Tifton, Georgia a Chinese restaurant offers a "vegetalian" dish. They always did have trouble with their L's and R's.)

Too bad that even when you ask in a Chinese restaurant, you can't always be sure of the answer. A waiter or a waitress, usually a young person will smile, excuse himself to get the answer from the cook, and then come back in a minute. What you may not know is that total immersion in English by serving as a waiter is how these kids learn our language. Hope he already understands you, because too often the cook speaks no English at all. Even if he does, he probably doesn't know the difference between vegetable, vegetarian, and vegetalian.

I hesitate to mention the reprehensible practice many Chinese restaurants have of flavoring everything with chicken stock. If you've been a vegetarian very long, you can tell which ones do. When you find one that doesn't, give them lots of business — you'll miss them if they fold.

I've had more vegetarian fun in Ethiopian restaurants than in any other kind. The first time it was a real surprise to find no silver on the table — this ancient culture may know better than we do that fingers were made before forks. The ones I've tried have plenty of dishes made from animals, but every one has a good selection of purely vegetarian items. To help with the finger feeding they do two things — cut up or puree everything into stews that require no knife and serve every meal with injera bread, large flat crepes folded into quarters and stacked on a platter. We were only neophytes long enough to watch the people at the next table tear off pieces of injera and pick up their food much like you pick a bug off the floor with a paper towel. By the time you eat it the injera is cold, but the stews are hot, and the combination is easy on the fingers and the palate.

The vegetarian stews are made from split peas and chick peas and beans and carrots and cabbage. Mustard is the only recognizable spice, but their many ethnic flavorings having exotic names, some hot in a spicy sense, are part of the fun.

Chinese and Italian restaurants abound, thankfully, or we vegetarians would be even more slender than we are. Other ethnic opportunities for those who don't eat animals are harder to find, but worth the search, including: Afgan, Ethiopian, Thai, Vietnamese, Middle Eastern, and, above all, Indian. Some yellow page restaurant listings have a listing by ethnic type at the end of the alphabetical list, saving time when you're in a strange city.

※※※

In our house, going out to eat is still a fun thing to do — almost as much fun as staying home and eating Charlene's cooking.

Food Labeling

Our first trip to the supermarket after becoming vegetarians instructed us in the complexities and duplicities of food labeling. We thought it would be simple to pick up what we wanted, check the ingredients lists, reject the animal components, and fill up the market basket. Dreamers! It took us more than twice as long as usual to get through the store hastily reading long paragraphs of unfamiliar, multisyllabic words set in print too small to read without glasses.

Several of our favorite items had to be left on the shelves because of beef flavoring, butter, whey, milk solids, and egg whites. Often these were items we might have guessed were vegetarian prior to reading the ingredients. We began to realize how often animal products are placed in ostensibly vegetable foods for flavoring or to stick them together or for who knows what other purposes. Take English muffins, for example. Our usual brand disclosed in the middle of its list of ingredients milk as a component. Adjacent on the same shelf was another brand made without milk. To get that one package we had to wade through two lists of ingredients. So we trudged through the store, picking up, reading, putting back, picking up and reading again. It was like shopping in quicksand.

Each succeeding trip to the store went better as we learned which products are acceptable without reading their packages. Today we read only the new items we want to try. Every so often I run across food packages with no list of ingredients. I wonder how these products escape the watchful eyes of the regulators who prescribe and enforce labeling practice. Perhaps there are exceptions written into the law, forced there by powerful lobbies who don't want their ingredients known, or perhaps the regulators just aren't very good at enforcement.

Whatever the reason, when I come across a package with no list, I wonder if there isn't something in there the public could perceive as dangerous.

Maybe being a vegetarian makes you paranoid. Even when there is a list of ingredients, I don't feel reassured that nothing dangerous is in the food. As the lists run on, you quickly pass all the recognizable food type ingredients and come to a bewildering and unpronounceable list of chemical names. Because they are toward the end of the list, I assume the quantity of these chemicals is small, but that is scant comfort, and I am left with many questions my faint memories of high school chemistry can't begin to answer. What's this stuff for? Is it a preservative, a pesticide, an insecticide, a homicide? Is it toxic or carcinogenic, and if not, has it ever been tested for toxicity or carcinogenesis, and if so were those tests on laboratory animals valid in predicting human reactions? Fat chance I'll ever get the answers to questions like this.

Maybe this is much ado about nothing. I'm sure every food producer will be quick to tell us either that these obscure chemicals are harmless or that they are used in such small quantities they have no effect on humans. But I eat some of these things every day. Are any of these ingredients fat soluble toxins which will accumulate in our tissues and kill us twenty years from now? I'll bet no one has conducted small dose tests of twenty years duration on humans unless our whole system of food supplies is a test and all of us are the laboratory animals.

Fifteen minutes in the kitchen cabinets provides me with more examples of chemical ingredients than I care to believe are in the food I eat. These compounds could be wholesome, beneficial, and healthy, but with names like sodium hexametaphosphate, why am I not reassured? Phosphates are big on these lists like sodium aluminum phosphate (aluminum?) and monocalcium phosphate. A container of candied pineapple lists $1/10$ of 1% benzoate of soda. If that stuff is OK to ingest, why are they so quick to emphasize how little of it they've included? The same container goes on to list sorbic acid and sulfur dioxide. Isn't sulfur dioxide one of those emissions gases of cars and power plants we're trying to legislate out of the atmosphere? What's it doing in my food?

Now come a more public spirited group of manufacturers who sense the problems we lay people have with chemical names and try to help us by gratuitously inserting little parenthetical explanations alongside certain obscure ingredients. A simple example is my jar of peanut butter listing mono and diglycerides parenthetically pointing out these are included "to promote creaminess." Scant solace to a veg like me who wants to avoid cream. Worse are a salad dressing containing calcium disodium edta (to improve flavor) and a can of kidney beans with disodium edta (preservative). All right, which is it fellas; is disodium edta for flavor or freshness, or is it really the same thing given enough time for lack of freshness to affect the flavor? And while we're at it, just what the hell is edta anyway? Granted these chemical names sound like so much sorcery to the average guy, but we all sleep easier at night thinking there must be some doctor level chemist out there not beholden to the food industry reading these labels and ready to blow the whistle if a really bad poison (can there be a good poison?) shows up on the list. Now with abbreviations like edta, even the chemists may not know what these things are. Food makers, spare me your parenthetical explanations; they sound like you're saying, "We know this stuff is dangerous, but if we don't put a little bit of it in, this package will be spoiled before you pick it off the shelf."

No discussion of ingredient lists would be complete without a comment on vitamins, those mysterious materials we cannot live without. Vitamins have some wild chemical names like the preservatives and fungicides. For example, vitamin B-1 is thiamine mononitrate, B-2 is riboflavin, and B-6 is pyridoxine hydrochloride. Man lived, flourished, and multiplied on this planet for more than two million years before he knew about vitamins and before he hung these names on them. Without help from vitamin pills, drug companies, pesticides, and preservatives, man progressed from an insignificant strain of animal life to the dominant species on earth, but today if you don't work at getting your RDA of all the vitamins and trace elements, you will surely experience nervous disorders, skin problems, bone weakness, or premature aging in the next couple of weeks. Thank you, medical science, for saving us from all those things, and thank you, food makers, for fortifying my crackers and soups with added vitamins. I hate to think of the wheelchair ridden, itching, shaking, basket case I'd be if I had to rely on the vitamins occurring naturally in my fruits, vegetables, nuts, and seeds.

Is it marketing or medicine that dictates adding the vitamins, or is it even more insidious? It could be an opportunity to add into ingredient lists some long, poisonous sounding chemical names which, on challenge, can be shown to be vitamins — those universally desirable, absolutely essential substances we all know are insepa-rable from life itself. Such challenges satisfied, then by extension, we can reason all these chemical compounds are all in there for our own good and to question them is only a cynical calculated attempt to destroy public faith in our food supply system.

Beyond people food, the premium priced, highly touted foods we buy for our dogs list some things I'd rather not think about like poultry by-product meal and poultry digest. I have visions of chicken feet and heads and whole baby male chicks complete with fuzzy feathers dumped unceremoniously into a cooker and steamed under pressure until when finished it leaves as a homogenous paste of biological material to be dried and pelletized. My dogs, carnivores that they are, don't seen to mind, but then they can't read the package.

All in all, ingredient lists make me sick.

✠✠✠

Labels also tabulate serving size, calories per serving, fat content, proteins, carbohydrates, cholesterol, and some vitamins and miner-als. The uniform format of this presentation is a dead giveaway these disclosures are required by law. Serious minded eaters want to know this stuff, especially if they are trying to limit fats, choles-terol, or calorie intake. The food makers, undaunted by the spirit and daunted only by the letter of the laws constraining them, have not let these requirements prevent them from presenting high fat, high calorie, and high cholesterol foods as low fat, low calorie, and low cholesterol. They simply reduce their "serving size." Thus a box of cocktail crackers I have describes the serving size as two crackers. These crackers are only slightly larger than a quarter and smaller than a half dollar, and a serving of two of these little bullets totals 60 calories. In my preveg days when I treated a table of hors d'oeuvres as more of a personal challenge than appetizers, I used two of these crackers sandwich style packed with $1/2$ inch of cream cheese or worse between them. And one of those babies wasn't a serving, it was a bite. The point here is that each of those crackers is 30 calories, and that's a lot when you're munching them down sequentially, but a "serving" of anything at only 60 calories seems like very few calories indeed.

Watch those ads for lean beef these days. Some are showing the serving size as three ounces. How long has it been since a three-ounce hamburger was enough for one of my meals? Probably since I learned to talk so I could tell Mom I was still hungry.

Unless you avoid animal foods, thereby avoiding most saturated fats, the cholesterol content shown on a food package is meaningless, because most of the body's cholesterol is synthesized from the saturated fats we eat — only a smaller portion results from the cholesterol in our food. But if you do avoid animal foods, the cholesterol is always zero. Food makers love cholesterol or the lack of it because everyone knows something about it and thinks he or she would like to avoid it. Hardly settling for a zero cholesterol item buried in the legally required list of food components, if a food has no cholesterol, the lablemakers print a bright band somewhere on the label shouting "zero cholesterol" or "cholesterol free." The food can be mostly coconut or palm oil or any of the saturated fats ready to cause a deadly buildup of blood cholesterol but these guys ballyhoo their no cholesterol status figuring, like P. T. Barnum, on a sucker's being born every minute. Thankfully some food makers are stopping this deceptive practice and the FDA has begun to jawbone against it.

Another area of abuse is the __% fat free type of labeling. Such claims almost always refer to the percent of fat by weight in a food, but most foods are mostly water by weight. Water, having no nutritional value, has nothing to do with how fatty a food is. Most vegetarians know the calories of fat as a percent of total calories is what counts. Keep it under 30% or down to as low as 10% if you're trying for an ultra low fat diet. You can figure the percent calories of fat from the label information, but they make it hard for you. Just remember each gram of fat is nine calories. This is one comparison they can't screw up with an unrealistic serving size — the percent fat comes out the same regardless of serving size.

Try to figure the real percent fat by calories for 3% butterfat milk or 93% fat free bologna and you'll have a better picture of a cynical system of public deception by lots of food makers. Don't hold your breath waiting for these guys to police themselves and adopt uniform, truthful, and informative standards for food labeling. And, sadly, don't expect government to step in and solve it either. Remember the labels we have now are the result of considerable legislation and regulation.

SECTION FOUR

HEALTH

Habits and Addictions

Feeding our faces is not only required to feed our bodies, it is usually a source of considerable pleasure. We have woven eating into nearly every leisure activity, from popcorn at the movies and hot dogs at the ball park to brats and beer at the local Octoberfest celebrations. At a carnival, elephant ears and funnel cakes and buffalo burgers and tacos and corn dogs and polish sausages and cheese nachos and more spew forth from open hatches in the sides of vendors' wagons rolled together like a gypsy caravan camped for the night. All that solid stuff is washed down with lemon shakeups and soda pop and beer and coffee mostly in the name of pleasure, not hunger. As a matter of fact, we don't usually even go to carnivals until after dinner.

Other social activities are structured around food for pleasure. Weddings have cakes and cocktail parties have little sandwiches of salmon paste and cheese and olives. Chafing dishes sizzling full of Vienna sausages and rumaki and compotes of shrimp cooling on beds of shaved ice come to mind. We play restaurant connoisseurs seeking out strange new cuisines more for the social experience — for the pleasure we desire — than for sustenance. Indeed, in a society where good food is relatively cheap and widely available, only society's outcasts associate food with curing hunger — for everyone else food is about pleasure, not hunger.

Little wonder then the typical nonveg, having been raised to think of meat as the *primary* course of every meal, and having come to associate eating that meat as a pleasurable activity, is disquieted when he is told the mainstays of his diet are the sources of heart disease, stroke, diabetes, kidney stones, etc. What a cruel twist of fate that something that feels so good can be bad for you, he thinks as he tries to reason his way around the incessant news linking *his* lifestyle with *his* early death. And just as the typical smoker has promised himself he'll cut down a little, the typical nonveg eventually corners his conscience and restores his peace of mind by deciding to trim off the fat, have fish once a week, eat more chicken, and have an oat bran muffin with his bacon and eggs. The exact dimensions of this conscience solution differ from person to person, but to a total vegetarian most of these "solutions" are distinctions without a real difference. The mere existence of such solutions does, however, betray the nonveg's subconscious knowledge of the harmful nature of animal based foods.

Nevertheless, the nonveg has now made peace with his mind and fortified himself to hear about still more studies linking animal foods with chronic disease and early death, comfortably believing he has made suitable changes in his own lifestyle and that he will live into his nineties finally quietly passing away in his sleep having retained an alert mind and a healthy glow to the last and never having experienced a sick day in his later life. It's a case of the pleasure centers of the brain triumphing over the intellect as they so often do with regard to smoking, sex, drugs, etc. Meat eating is at best a habit, at worst an addiction.

✠✠✠

I don't claim to understand the technical definitions of habits and addictions, but I am as comfortable with the terms in their general use in our language as the next guy. My own experience with smoking and quitting taught me what an addiction is. From ages 18 to 26 I was a heavy smoker working up to three packs a day. I can remember the battles in my head between my pleasure centers and my conscience as I thought about quitting. Those battles went on for months after I actually did quit like soldiers on the front lines who hadn't heard about an armistice. The only good smoking ever did for me was to give me an object lesson in addiction, and it isn't a pretty picture.

As I lived through addiction to nicotine, it had three primary elements:

1. An admittedly harmful activity perpetuated by the pleasure associated with it, real or imagined.

2. A fear of existing without that pleasure.

3. An extended period of physical pain and mental anguish associated with withdrawal.

More than 30 years have passed since I quit, but my memories of smoking and quitting are as clear as if I quit last year. My mental turmoil leading up to the decision to quit was unquenched by all the half measures I had tried — cutting down, low tar cigarettes, filters, etc. It burned on inside my head like a peat bog — constant, hot, refusing to be ignored. Fueling the debate were the values instilled by my parents, nonsmokers who, on this subject alone, were Puritanical. In the early 1960's less was known about smoking and the Surgeon General's warnings had not yet been placed on the packages, but even then stories linked it with cancer, heart trouble, gravelly voices, and leathery skin. I couldn't avoid hearing them, and they only harmonized with Mom and Dad's voices that had guided my childhood and were still echoing in my head. I fought back, protecting my pleasure, and procrastinated, running through every half measure I could think of, and I always came back to the same point — I had to smoke three packs a day of full strength cigarettes to be comfortable!

I would go to bed at night feeling smoked out, and I recall telling friends that if I could wake up feeling as badly as I did at bedtime, I'd never start smoking in the morning, but it never happened that way. That first cigarette after breakfast with coffee was always a pleasure I couldn't forego. Reason, science, upbringing, or ill effects, none of these could convince this smoker to kick the habit or, more correctly, break the addiction. What worked for me finally was fear.

My best friend's dad died suddenly in his late 50's. It was a heart attack, and he had been a cigarette smoker his whole life as was his son — one of the peers whose example had been a factor in my starting smoking. The day I went to the funeral, my mental forces for good were joined by a clairvoyant flash of fear as I imagined myself in my 50's still looking fairly young lying dead of the effects of smoking. Finally a bigger fear had overcome my fear of living without the pleasure. There was no escaping it. I quit that afternoon.

Then began months more of mental debate about starting again! I had thought breaking away would be the worst part, but staying away was the worst. While these new debates came at less frequent intervals, each time one surfaced I was only a striking match away from again having that same destructive monkey on my back. I found myself after six months away from cigarettes almost losing one of these debates — it had been weeks since the previous one. What saved me was a sense of all the pain I had endured to get that far. It was too big an investment to throw away even for the seductive anticipated pleasure of a cigarette. After going through that line of reasoning, I never wanted a cigarette again, and I really knew what addiction was all about.

❉❉❉

My departure from eating animal products was no less abrupt— my wife, Charlene, and I decided to do it between lunch and dinner one day. We quit totally — meat, eggs, dairy — and we never went back. I expected the same sort of mental battles and long withdrawal period from meat as I had with smoking years before, but I was amazed how easily I got through the transition. Frankly, neither of us ever again craved meat, although an occasional yen for cheese persisted for a few months. I recall the smoke from a barbecue restaurant would stimulate me momentarily, but that hunger could be satisfied by any food. Now, three years later, the barbecue smoke is not pleasant, and it certainly doesn't make me hungry.

The only desire left from my meat eating days is a mechanical one — I still long for something to sink my incisors into. Today the meat substitutes like tofu, tempeh, seitan, and certain vegetables like eggplant and mushrooms usually satisfy that craving. All things considered, no pain attended our transition from nonveg to a totally vegetarian lifestyle, so neither of us really went through a "withdrawal" from meat.

This lack of withdrawal symptoms upon becoming vegetarian is a common experience. A number of vegetarian friends have told me they had no overhanging desire for the taste of meat when they changed. To be sure, some vegetarians have returned to meat eating and some have cycled back and forth more than once, but those who returned to meat sometimes did so because of their spouses or their difficulty in finding a variety of good vegetarian food at restaurants. Meat craving after withdrawal doesn't seem to be a factor.

I conclude, therefore, that meat eating is a habit, rather than an addiction for most people. It is associated with pleasure and the fear of doing without it, but for most people it does not produce the severe withdrawal symptoms associated with addictions. The good news, then, is as a habit meat eating is easier to stop than a true addiction. The bad news is a habit as widely ingrained as meat eating will likely be practiced by most people for a long time to come.

This Cholesterol Business

Not every one of us has a cholesterol problem, but too many of us do. Most of us don't have a dad who died early, still a seemingly healthy and active man, but I did. I took twenty years to pick up on this clue to my hereditary cholesterol problem and do something about it—twenty years of fooling myself about my health.

Dad died in 1968 at the age of 67. Those who knew him just before that electrifying event never imagined he had any kind of a health problem. He didn't know it himself, because coronary artery disease is a "feel good" disease, often producing no symptoms at all until it is too late. Happily retired to his bayfront home in southwestern Florida, Dad filled his days with woodworking, yard maintenance, and fooling around with his boat. He fished and entertained his friends on the boat and seemed to all of us to be a model retiree. Illness, to the extent it would ever affect him, seemed decades ahead even while he lived out his last few days.

About a week before he died, Dad began to have a little insomnia. Nothing much to worry about, he and Mom reasoned, but it left him feeling tired during the days. A couple of days later he noticed some stomach distress (or so it seemed) and, true to his ethic about taking care of himself, he sought the advice of a doctor. In those days in small Florida towns you couldn't count on getting quality medical care, and the doctor confidently diagnosed ulcers and prescribed a bland diet.

My last telephone conversation with Dad was on the subject of ulcers. I had earlier had a mild colitis condition (probably brought on by martinis at cocktail hour) and lived through the same kind of bland diet now in store for Dad. "Dad, you'll really enjoy it if you set your mind to it," I counseled, remembering my earlier diet of poached eggs, much milk, and mashed potatoes. "Just watch the salt and you'll be fine." Ulcers were a real surprise to Dad and everyone else in the family. How could he live through a working lifetime of responsible jobs including managing over 400 people in a factory, all the time avoiding ulcers, and now have them after five years of carefree retired life?

In retrospect, the answer is easy. He didn't have ulcers, he was building up to a heart attack. It came one week after the sleeplessness began. The same day, my first wife and one small son had arrived for a visit. He had been too tired to go up to the airport to meet them. By evening, feeling a little better, he ate dinner and went out in the yard to secure the lines on his small fishing boat. That was the last thing he ever did. Going to bed for a rest, he said goodnight to everyone, and it turned out to be goodbye. In bed, he was gone the minute it hit him, and the desperate efforts to wake him, revive him, call emergency were all useless. As I flew south through that sad night, it was hard to believe he was gone, but he was — inescapably, irretrievably — gone.

Today my curiosity still irritates me asking, "What was his cholesterol level?" Though no records exist to tell me, I know it was high, perhaps well over 300. I've learned about hypercholesterolemia, my disease and his; I've learned its many forms and my particular type; and I've learned how this genetic defect passes from parents to children, particularly hitting the males. Killer cholesterol is constant as it affects the generations, but what we know about it and what we can do about it has changed from Dad's time to mine.

If your cholesterol level is over 200, and particularly if you are a male with a family history of heart disease, you have a much elevated risk of heart disease yourself. Deposits of material are building up inside your arteries and veins, gradually making their passages smaller. The condition is so common and so widely discussed in the U.S. today, most of us know our cholesterol levels and many of us try to cut down on some of the foods which raise cholesterol levels. In Dad's day, doctors thought a level of 300 (now considered dangerous) was nothing to worry about.

I had been told as a late teen or young adult that my cholesterol was around 300, but not to worry unless it went well above 300. When I brought that news home to my parents, Mom, who knew her level, said hers was about the same, and Dad, who didn't know his, said nothing. For a short time after that I tried to watch the number of eggs I ate, but it was a halfhearted effort gradually pushed back into my subconscious. After all, if I wasn't alarmingly over 300 and the doctors weren't worried, why should I be? From then until much later when I seriously addressed my cholesterol problem (a few months after becoming a vegetarian), I actually thought my higher levels came from Mom's side. The creeping doubts that came into my mind after Dad's unexpected death were balanced year by year with a growing confidence about Mom's advancing age. I had developed a convenient little mental lock on the situation, keeping me from conscience problems and from doing anything about it. By the time I was in my fifties and she was further into her eighties, I kept reassuring myself how little her high cholesterol had to do with her longevity — an argument that seemed more forceful as each year went by. Talk about fooling yourself!

I devised still other ways to ignore my cholesterol. We've all heard of "good cholesterol" (meaning high density lipoprotein, HDL) and "bad cholesterol" (meaning low density lipoprotein, LDL). I thought Mom's high level must contain a health promoting higher proportion of good HDL or she wouldn't have lived to be so old. While I knew the only way to be sure about my own condition was to have a complete blood lipid profile run showing HDL, LDL, and triglyceride levels, I procrastinated continuing to believe Mom's good health equated to my good health. I didn't have a complete lipid profile done until I was nearly 55 and already a vegetarian.

About three years before that I had taken a stress test as a part of our company's executive health program. I blew into tubes, gave blood for tests, had an EKG, and, hooked up to a dozen wires, worked out on a treadmill. The report came back that I had very good lung function despite minor lung surgery done many years before. They noted my cholesterol was high at 286 and suggested I go to a specialist to treat that condition. I took the good parts of the results to heart but ignored the suggestion to look into my cholesterol level. After all, I had worked my way through all that based on Mom's longevity.

Two years later I repeated the stress test just after turning 54. This time they could show by comparison a reduction in capability of my cardiopulmonary system — I had given up on the treadmill sooner. All of the other tests hardly changed. Still the cholesterol count was high (about 290), and they still recommended seeing a specialist. I was six months away from becoming a vegetarian, but of course I didn't know it.

I had expected another good report before going in for that test, but now they were saying they could measure a deterioration in my cardiopulmonary system. I thought about eating better, getting more exercise, and reducing my stress levels, but I really didn't do anything to help myself until, months later, I made the sudden switch to being a vegetarian.

My growing worries about my own health, stimulated by the declining stress test results and a developing suspicion that on matters of heart health I was more my father's than my mother's son, all helped me to receive and accept the vegetarian messages I got the following June at the Symposium of the National Alliance for Animals. Being a vegetarian, I thought, could be my answer — a way to clear two of my guilty consciences: the one about my health and the other about the suffering animals.

My new vegetarian lifestyle became my latest reason to feel good about myself. This time it was a valid reason — one that worked and made a positive difference in my health. Pounds fell away, I looked and felt better, and I was certain my cholesterol level must be coming down. After about four months of this new life, I decided to seek out medical proof of my progress — another manifestation of a continuing need to feel good about myself. This time, for economy, I went to a suburban supermarket where one of the big Cincinnati hospitals was doing cholesterol screening for just a few dollars. Twenty minutes later, I had the results.

Four months of vegetarian life had reduced my cholesterol from over 290 to 224, an encouraging change but not enough to put me into the safe category, now well understood to be below 200. The literature I got at that screening test promoted a more complete evaluation by the hospital's cholesterol center for people at my level. I could no longer escape the obvious — I needed help — so I went in.

I had to fast for 12 hours before my first visit to the center, a requirement for a complete lipid profile. In my consultation with the doctor I told him about the stress tests and my total vegetarian status for the last four months. He asked about my family history, particularly noting Dad's age at and cause of death. Even though it would be a day or so before the complete lipid profile was available, he told me I would definitely be placed on some drug therapy to reduce blood cholesterol levels. He explained they nearly always try dietary modification first, but my four months as a total vegetarian had already given me all the reduction I could expect from diet alone and that at 224, my level was still too high to accept without intervention. He shocked me when, in answer to my question, he guessed I had lost about 40 percent of the area of my coronary arteries.

Although this cholesterol center treats 1000 patients, I'm sure only a few have as good a diet, cholesterol-wise, as I have. With the absolute elimination of dietary cholesterol and saturated animal fats and the higher fiber content of my all vegetarian fare, few of those 1000 people can match my self help in nutrition. Still I needed the nutritional counseling, as they helped me to recognize unnecessary fats in my diet, weeded out highly saturated vegetable foods like coconut and palm oil and chocolate, and helped me to make optimal choices of margarine, cooking oils, etc. Watching my daily food diaries, they also verified I was getting a balanced array of plant foods. Eventually the nutritional counseling became repetitive, and I could be weaned away from it.

My cholesterol doctor was aware of the potential for vitamin B-12 deficiency in my diet. Most vegetarians make light of the issue and I've even heard some say we store several years' worth in our bodies. We decided to check my B-12 levels as a regular addition to my blood tests. Surprise, surprise, I tested deficient in B-12 after only six months as a vegetarian, a problem then handled inexpensively by a daily B-12 supplement pill. Subsequent tests verified the level is no longer deficient, and the B-12 test is now run only occasionally as a check.

The medical treatment began soon after the first complete blood profile was run. I was placed on a drug known as Lopid, generically called gemfibrizol. Lopid acts primarily to raise HDL which addresses my particular type of cholesterol problem — an inability to make enough HDL. HDL searches through your vascular system and acts to remove the deposited materials resulting from the LDL. My lack of enough HDL was the real cause of my high cholesterol count.

At the beginning of my therapy, we had set a goal to bring my total count down to 180 or lower. The doctor had explained at that level new research suggested actual regression of cholesterol deposits on the arterial walls takes place. Fantastic, I thought, it could be possible to reverse the bad effects of all those years of eating animals. Maybe it was not too late to do something right about my health after all.

My impatience to attain the 180 level grew thin when, after several months on Lopid, HDL had risen slightly, but the total count was still over 200. I wanted 180, and I wasn't getting there fast enough to suit me. Besides this, Lopid had the side effect of occasionally causing sleeplessness. As I shared my reservations about Lopid with the doctor, he showed a willingness to switch me to a different drug, Mevacor — generically known as lovastatin. Mevacor was a newer drug, but its earliest patients were years ahead of me in their experience, and their experience had been phenomenal. Total cholesterol counts of Mevacor patients can drop as much as 30 percent because of the drug. Happily it worked on me as well, and my last total count was 158. Also, in the two years I've been taking Mevacor, more clinical research has confirmed the regression potential for people with counts lowered below 180.

Whether my own arterial cholesterol deposits are regressing or not, only involved and unwarranted tests can tell. It seems certain, nevertheless, I'm not building up my deposits, so at least I've halted the progress of heart disease. Statistically, I've reduced my chances of dying from heart disease by large percentages based on the big drop in my LDL and the slight rise in my HDL.

Looking back, I can see how I only went to the doctor when I thought I would get a good report. Apart from the considerable direct health benefits I get from being a total vegetarian, I think that lifestyle was responsible for getting me started on my cholesterol therapy. If I had not become a vegetarian, I might still be fooling myself about my high cholesterol count.

Am I the only one who fools himself? Absolutely not. About a year ago, I had written a column critical of the egg because of its cholesterol and saturated fat content. It was the one where I called eggs capsules of death. I got a letter from a lady who loved her eggs as much as I used to. She displayed her own twisted reasoning when she acknowledged they were high in cholesterol, but asked how anyone could be sure they weren't high in the good kind of cholesterol, proving, as we all do from time to time, that a little bit of knowledge can be a dangerous thing.

More On Mom

I've already written lots about Mom, who was an unknowing source of my vegetarian life. She's gone now, but fondly remembered by everyone who knew her well. I was lucky to have had her for fifty-seven years. After my dad died more than twenty years ago, I think I knew her better than anyone, and perhaps I remember her better than anyone. How different was our relationship in its last twenty years than it was in its first twenty years.

Mom was the authoritarian in our family. I only recall corporal punishment from Dad once or twice in my life, but as a young man I used to tell Mom that I could recall her spanking me every day when I was little. In reality, no one kept a journal of spankings in our house, and I'm sure my "every day" charge was exaggerated and unfair to her. She'd smile when I said that and not argue, knowing it didn't make any difference once I was grown up. Although I probably earned a spanking every day as a little kid, I'll bet I only got about one out of every seven I needed.

Today we have a cartoon in our paper called Calvin and Hobbes. Calvin is a cute little kid, wise beyond his years and bent on breaking every rule and trying every idea, no matter how wild. Hobbes is his teddy tiger, a real foil for Calvin in his imagination. I skip most comics, particularly the dramatic ones. Calvin, nevertheless, is my all time favorite, because he evokes memories of the many escapades, adventures, and punishments I had as a kid. He never gets away with anything bad, any more than I did. His parents are trying to insure he grows up into a responsible adult, just as mine tried. Life in his family is a constant tug of war between his overactive imagination and the stability imposed by Mom and Dad, especially Mom — just as it was in my family.

At the time Dad died, Mom was in her late sixties, still showing that same independence and strength she had when we were small. She seldom asked for or needed help, and in her first months of widowhood, with no help from anyone, she sold their real property advantageously and selected an apartment in a nearby town where she resided happily for the the remaining twenty-two years of her life. When she moved, Jean and I lived far away, so we were no help in selling off excess belongings, disposing of Dad's things, packing for the move, and arranging the details — she did it all herself.

Mom's new apartment was on the first floor of a large new building located about three blocks away from a small shopping district. Once settled in, she began to do her shopping by walking to the stores, and she was uptown most days. I've always been a great believer in walking as exercise, and Mom's new level of physical activity as she approached seventy years old made me feel proud. I don't think she was ever healthier or looking better than she was in those years when she walked to do her shopping.

Well before she reached seventy-five, Mom's lifelong meat eating diet began to catch up to her. She always had one hip elevated an inch higher than the other, but it had not caused her problems in her younger years. Her active lifestyle protected her for many years, but now skeletal changes caused her to have pains in her legs, hips, and back. A doctor decided that a shoe lift on one side would adjust her skeleton well enough to eliminate the pain. It was a good common sense answer, but it wasn't the answer for Mom.

Mom was a shoe freak, having at least fifty pairs. In Florida, where anything stored for long can mildew, Mom knew how to protect her shoes. They were all displayed in stacked clear plastic shoe boxes on the shelf of her extra large closet. She could be stubborn when she wanted to, and she mentally rejected the shoe lift from the beginning. She would never expose to the rest of the family that she wasn't following doctor's orders, and none of us lived close enough to check up on her very often, so we had to assume she was wearing the lift. When we'd ask her on the phone, she'd say, "sometimes, not always." That was a white lie; she should have said, "seldom, or almost never."

Mom's gaggle of shoeboxes was used as an excuse for not wearing the lift. She'd wear it one day, leave it in a shoe, and a few days later, the only way to find it was to go through all the shoes. When we came through for vacation, we'd find the lift, but it would get lost again as soon as we were gone. I'm sure Mom wished she had never gone to that doctor or at least that we'd never learned about the lift. We finally gave up, and I know she threw it away.

Unfortunately no lift meant no cure to her pains, so she compensated by walking less. She cut down the number of shopping trips and did most of them driving her car. I have always believed that her health during her widowhood was directly proportional to her walking, and the facts seem to bear out this lay person's medical opinion. As she became less active, her skeleton escalated the war it was waging on her. Year by year you could see her bend over more. She was only 5 feet 2 inches tall to begin with, but by the time of her death, she was barely five feet tall. Shortening was not due to compression of the cartilage discs in her spine, it was due to its curving forward — osteoporosis.

As she bent forward, her balance also grew worse, and by her late seventies she had begun to have occasional falls. The collection of shoes evolved, almost against her will, into an equally large collection of shoes with lower heels. As we had earlier nagged her about the lift, we now found ourselves nagging her about the height of her heels. Mom hated low heels, having always been short, but this woman wasn't dense - she knew she could kill herself in a fall. She did buy shoes with lower heels than she had bought before, and she hated having to do it. We, on the other hand, looked at the newer shoes and thought the heels were still too high. She never got them as low as we'd like, but they were all too low in her mind.

By the age of eighty, she had begun to have falls, sometimes resulting in broken bones. The falls were alarming to Jean and me, and several times in her last ten years we flew through the night to her hospital bedside to hear some doctor explain which bones she had broken and how long she'd need live-in help to recuperate. In addition, a bout with intestinal cancer at age eighty required five weeks in a hospital and percipitated another operation several years later for related adhesions. Finally, a number of falls not resulting in breaks reminded us how poor her balance system had become.

As osteoporosis progressed, her activity declined further. She now shopped only rarely, always going in her car. She never walked anywhere except around her apartment and to and from her car. Her driving wasn't bad for someone in her late eighties, and it was ever so much better than her walking.

Mom feared falls as much as we did. She understood how her own dad had died of complications following a broken hip, and she'd had enough falls and breaks to know how fragile she was. She tried to be careful because in addition to the trauma of falls, she disliked having someone living in her home with her while she mended. Her independence was her most prized possession. Trying to help herself, she had been drinking milk on a regular basis for more than twenty years hoping she was adding calcium to her body. She also always had plenty of vegetables for the vitamins and calcium they contain, but she was also still a meat eater, having it at least twice a day. Her style of cooking, which I had loved as a kid, used plenty of animal fat in gravies, sauces, vegetable dishes — in nearly any dish she prepared.

For the last two and a half years of her life, my education as a vegetarian helped me to understand what was happening to poor Mom. In her valiant efforts to eat well rounded meals (by commonly accepted nonveg standards) and take on extra calcium, particularly by drinking milk, she was overdosing herself with protein. Instead of adding calcium, her milk and meat and cheese and butter were actually robbing her frail bones of their calcium day by day. Like thousands, perhaps millions of other older women, through misinformation in the marketing of animal foods she had been led down the garden path. It's only my guess, but I suspect those same animal foods led to an increasingly clogged vascular system destroying the operation of the tiny balance sensors in her ears designed to kept her upright. As I came to know more about such things, it was obviously way too late to make a difference in Mom's life.

Two falls in rapid succession eventually proved fatal for Mom. The first was a head injury and broke out a few teeth. It also cracked a wrist bone, but she rebounded well and was home living independently again ten days later when a second fall broke her hip forcing her entry into the hospital. She never went home again.

The head injury from the first fall had started giving her focal seizures, preventing setting the hip fracture. The seizure medicine was hard on her and she was in intensive care on a monitor for days as we watched vital measurements grow weaker and weaker. Then, miraculously, she rallied, left intensive care, and even left the hospital for a nursing home where a general decline began. Six days after entering the nursing home and forty days after the first fall, she died.

She died at about the same time in the afternoon I had been born. I noticed because she died on my fifty-seventh birthday.

On Longevity

Thinking about my own predispositions to chronic disease and looking back at the fates of my own ancestors, I find longevity on both sides of the family, but nevertheless, I discover a litany of the chronic diseases rampant in western society.

Barring accidents, pestilence, and malevolence, longevity seems to be related to family background (or where you got what you have) and how you live (or what you do with what you have). In the former category, most of us take an interest in the health problems of our recent ancestors. We can do nothing to change our genetic makeup — our possible predispositions to heart disease or diabetes or what have you — but once suspecting such predispositions in ourselves, we can then work in the second category (what we do with what we have) to minimize possible dangers to our lives.

Dad's father also died of a heart attack in his later seventies, up to the end a seemingly healthy man. His mother lived into her early eighties and died of circulatory problems affecting her legs. She never had an amputation, but she was close to that drastic step when she died. One of Dad's sisters had Alzheimer's disease, making it into her mid-eighties, and his other sister is alive today well into her nineties. A brother, who abused himself with alcohol and tobacco his entire adult life, was about ninety when he died. My Dad was the only one in large family to die so early; he clearly had that defective cholesterol gene and his siblings didn't.

On Mom's side is another tale of longevity. She lived past eighty-nine dying of complications from a nasty fall, but really she was killed by her osteoporosis. Her mother died in her mid-seventies of a heart attack as she was leaving a hospital after an abdominal cancer operation. She had had diabetes for years. Mom's father lived past ninety dying from a thromboembolism developing after a fall dealt him a broken hip. Grandpa was also senile when he died. One of Mom's brothers was in his late fifties when lung cancer took him. Her other brother lived into his eighties, and he had diabetes like his mother.

With all that longevity on both sides, why should I worry? Unfortunately, I finally came to understand the most important hereditary factor affecting my own longevity was Dad's heart disease along with his inferred and my well known propensity for elevated cholesterol. But I'm also struck by the causes of death of several people in the previous two generations of my family. Consider circulatory problems, balance problems, osteoporosis, diabetes, Alzheimer's disease, senility, intestinal cancer, and heart disease. Except for my uncle's lung cancer, obviously linked to his years of cigarette smoking, they all suffered from and died of things which could have been prevented or minimized by vegetarian lifestyles. While no one can say how each of them would have fared as vegetarians, it seems reasonable their individual fates would have been different if they had avoided animal foods, and I can't escape the feeling they would have lived even longer.

I see no way the uncle who died from lung cancer could have avoided that protracted, painful, and early exit from life short of not smoking — diet wouldn't have prevented his disease. But for all the others, the opposite is true. I'll leave it to John Robbins in his wonderful book, *Diet for a New America*, to demonstrate the connections between animal foods and the diseases of my ancestors. He easily convinced me.

I'll never know what would have happened to my ancestors as vegetarians, but I fully intend to find out what my own fate will be as one who abstains from all animal foods. My prescription for protecting and extending the life of yours truly is to stick with the cholesterol therapy as a defense against the biggest danger, heart disease, and stick with vegetarian life for that reason as well as to ward off those other maladies that caught up with my grandparents, parents, and aunts and uncles.

✠✠✠

Even vegetarians don't live forever, but they do have much better track records than the animal eaters do.

More On Longevity

Antivivisectionism is a word I learned as a kid, not because I was interested it, but because it had so many syllables. Until I became interested in animal protection, I ignored the subject. Once I listened to the arguments against using animals in medical research, I began to understand how few of the great strides man has made in extending his own lifespan have been provided by medical science as it is being promoted to us today. One book, *The Cruel Deception* by Dr. Robert Sharpe, gave me a much better understanding of how little we have received and how little we can really expect from medical science. I am now a certified cynic on the subject, believing the best hope we all have for a long and healthy life comes from preventive measures we take ourselves, not from a bunch of overpriced practitioners trained to address our symptoms when it is already too late. Little hope either is offered by the drug companies, the societies begging funds for medical research, or the expensive, relatively unproductive National Institutes for this and that we all pay for through taxes. I make these statements fully recognizing the huge increases we have experienced in human lifespan.

On the subject of lifespan, this week I read that a baby girl born today can expect, on the average, to attain an age of eighty years. All my life I've considered anyone who reached eighty to have beaten the odds, but now, apparently, it's just coming out even. Not too many generations ago if you reached eighty you had not only beaten the odds, you had run away with the crap table and the banker's money.

In Christ's time to live past your thirties was an accomplishment, and even in colonial America getting into your fifties required a rare combination of a robust constitution, great care, and lots of luck. One hundred years later, about 1850, the odds against a long life hadn't changed much. Those times were saturated with too many infant and childhood deaths and a fearsome array of infectious diseases like smallpox, measles, diphtheria, and cholera sometimes wiping out thousands in epidemics. Medical practice in the early nineteenth century was a largely ineffective collection of home cures, old wives' tales, and crude, often unanesthetized surgical experiments performed by doctors who had learned on cadavers snatched from graves.

The biggest gains in human life expectancy came between 1850 and 1950. By that time, a man could expect to live into his late sixties. During that century of progress the infectious or acute diseases were beaten back until they were hardly considered threats to life anymore. Science was responsible for this great leap forward in the human condition, but it wasn't the kind of medical science we are being sold today. It wasn't researchers testing medicines on animals and people in clinics or wizards in laboratories full of glass retorts, condensation columns, and Bunsen burners. It wasn't companies and men of science armed with microscopes and centrifuges developing pills and capsules and injections full of miracle drugs — silver bullets able to wipe those man killing microbes off the face of the earth. Most of us antivivisectionists know better. Most of us know the answers came from the more productive, but less dramatic fields of sanitation, ventilation, and perhaps even nutrition.

While sanitation and ventilation are so widely understood today we almost take them for granted, these subjects were hardly understood in the eighteenth and early nineteenth centuries. In 1854 a cholera epidemic in London was nipped in the bud by a clever man who removed the handle from a pump at a communal well. Medicine wasn't involved, just astute deduction once most of the sufferers were found to have used the well. Indoor plumbing, community sewage treatment systems, central heating and ventilating systems, personal cleanliness, and better cleaning and cooking of foods all made contributions to the increase in lifespan. As 1950 approached, vaccines, inoculations, and drugs helped, but the acute diseases were already largely conquered by the vastly improved sanitary practices in western societies.

With infectious diseases well controlled, longer-lived man began to suffer more often from chronic diseases like heart disease, stroke, cancer, and diabetes. These killers had always existed and indeed often took the "lucky" ones outliving the averages, but they didn't become the primary threats they are today until most infectious diseases were controlled and most people were living long enough to come down with the chronic diseases. Since 1950 medical science has directed huge, largely unsucessful efforts toward "cures" for these chronic diseases. We have a war on cancer declared by President Nixon and still to be won. We attack heart disease with every weapon available — laboratories, computers, animal experiments, clinical studies, and surgery, but the silver bullets elude us decade after decade. Some say there is more cancer now than when the war on cancer was declared, so maybe we're losing that war. And it would be hard to make a believable case we are winning the battle against heart disease.

Diet for a New America discusses nearly every major chronic disease we have left, presenting convincing evidence that each could be better resisted by a vegetarian than by a nonveg. In a very real sense, our advances in lifespan have added an entire range of health arguments in favor of vegetarian eating, arguments that didn't really motivate vegetarian practice when men lived much shorter lives. Add in an antivivisectionist's understanding of the weak promise offered by medical science and the case for vegetarian eating is all the more compelling.

SECTION FIVE

ANIMALS AND HUNTING

The Making of
an Animal Person

Not long after Charlene and I were married, we acted on my desire to have a place in the country and acquired a farm in southern Indiana along the Ohio River. It was about about 50 miles away from Cincinnati where we lived and I worked, and we planned to use it as a weekend retreat from our busy city life. Finding that old farm, a little over 100 acres of hills and woods with a few open hayfields, was a milestone in the development of our feelings about animals. Not that this was a farm for raising animals anymore — it was retired when we got it, just recreation space. We rehabilitated the old farmhouse and began spending our weekends there, soon becoming fascinated with the deer, fox, birds, and other forms of life around us.

While the house was still torn apart, our first dog adopted us. Annie was a stray Beagle, less than a year old and very hungry. We couldn't turn her away, and today, ten years later, she is still with us. As much as I love to tell them, the stories of each of the dogs and cats we collected into our lives would crowd this book. It is sufficient to say they were all strays who came along and adopted us. We placed into good homes some along the way, but five great dogs and five lovable cats share our lives today.

Until about 1986 we were animal lovers but certainly not educated about animal rights and animal protection. Then a Cincinnati newspaper carried a story about a county dog pound near the farm, telling of neglect and starvation at the hands of an inept Indiana sheriff's department which didn't want the animal control function anyway.

The same sort of neglect in the same county had made the city newspapers a few years before. As it happened that county was where Charlene had grown up and where her mother still lived — about midway between our city home and our weekend farm retreat.

We had been members, although inactive, of the local humane society in that county, and we decided to attend their next meeting to see what could be done about the pound problems. The meeting told us lots about why there hadn't been much progress locally for the animals. About a half dozen regulars came to the meeting and talked about how awful the dog pound was, but couldn't decide on a course of action to address the problems. We showed up with a few ideas and suggestions, but each was met with a reply something like, "We've tried that in the past, and it won't work." Admittedly, our ideas weren't great, but after the meeting, Charlene and I looked at each other and said, "No wonder things don't change very fast around here."

One ray of hope developed at the meeting. The next monthly meeting of the Humane Society would be a special public meeting to discuss the county's dog pound problems. With this, Charlene shifted into high gear, and I was willingly dragged along into our first exercise in activism for the animals. Plans for the public meeting monopolized our conversations every dinner hour and evening. Charlene founded an entity she called Friends of the County Animal Shelter and made plans to present a proposal to the public meeting. As luck would have it, her Mom lived on the busy highway between the two largest towns in the county. 50,000 cars a day passed her house. We rented a flashing trailer sign to promote the meeting, and began calling civic leaders and the media to build attendance.

The city paper's coverage of the pound atrocities had opened the public's eyes, assuring that the American Legion Hall was full for the meeting. Two Cincinnati television stations covered the event. During the meeting, the sheriff, some of the county commissioners, and several citizens got up and talked. Charlene proposed to lead a group, study the problem, and make recommendations to the commissioners regarding the pound and the animal control function. Her proposal was adopted without opposition by those present, and we were off and running.

The group she formed had Humane Society members, a veterinarian, a local business leader, and a county commissioner. They met several times and eventually concluded that a comprehensive animal control ordinance should be adopted by the county commission. The ordinance would establish a legal requirement to care for pound animals responsibly, set standards for their care, feeding, and disposition, and establish an appointed animal control commission to oversee the county's animal control functions. The Great Lakes Regional Office of the Humane Society of the United States became an important resource, supplying us with sample ordinances, literature on shelter operation, and copious consultation over the phone.

Concurrently the Friends group began to raise funds for a better shelter and collected signatures for a petition to the county commission urging passage of an animal control ordinance. We attended street fairs in search of signatures, produced hundreds of posters placing them in store windows all over the county, and in Charlene's name, I ghosted several long tracts for the local weekly paper to be run as advertisements to raise public consciousness and focus the attention of the political leaders. The petition with more than 2000 signatures was presented to the commissioners, and the newspaper ads made sure the entire county was well informed about the need for an ordinance. We were nevertheless concerned about the commissioners' seeming reluctance to change anything in the county government, and we thought they would avoid enacting an ordinance if public attention waned.

The commissioners scheduled a public hearing on the draft ordinance the Friends had proposed, and we expected them to try to table the matter after hearing from several "arranged" opposing statements. We began planning, therefore, to be sure that no one could ever characterize the hearing as anything but an overwhelming expression of public sentiment in favor of the ordinance. We invited Sandy Rowland, our Regional Office Director of the Humane Society of the United States to speak for the ordinance, and planned for the statements of several proponents.

The hearing room used by the commissioners is a well designed, modern room capable of seating about 100 comfortably. The audience partly encircles the commissioners' desk in a series of elevated rows of seats, theater style. The night of the hearing on the animal control ordinance, more than 140 people crowded into the room including some Cincinnati television news cameras. Although about three or four months had passed since this all began, we had kept the pound problems a hot topic with the public. Because we sensed a huge majority was in favor of the ordinance, we took one other step to try to prevent the matter from being tabled until it was forgotten. I think it was the straw that broke the back of the commissioners' reluctance to do anything for the animals.

We prepared large tags with adhesive backing on fluorescent orange paper. The 3 by 5 inch tags had large black letters saying simply, FOR THE ORDINANCE. We stationed volunteers at the doors to the county building to offer the tags to everyone who entered. Imagine our delight when nearly everyone who entered took one to wear. Imagine the commissioners reaction when they filed into the crowded room, sat down at their desk, looked out at the audience, and and found themselves surrounded by a sea of orange posters pasted to nearly every shirt, coat, blouse, and sweater. As I stood near the desk and looked back at the audience, I had to search to find the few who weren't wearing badges. Less than ten would be about the right count. The public will was not going to be misconstrued on this issue.

Indeed a few arranged speakers opposed the ordinance, but we had arranged better speakers in favor. Sandy Rowland gave one of the best statements in favor of responsible, humane animal control I've ever heard. At the end of the evening, we all knew the commissioners would act, and after a short period for consideration, the ordinance was adopted. Some equivocating amendments were added since then, but the county today has a much improved animal control function, a watchdog commission, a new sheriff who clearly recognizes his responsibility for animal control, and a public who can breathe somewhat easier.

The time for dissolving the Friends group and encouraging the local humane society had arrived. Funds collected for a new shelter were added to those of the society, a new board and officers were elected, and an ongoing fundraising program for a new shelter began. The county pledged land and a substantial contribution, and a new shelter has just been completed.

The local humane society has undergone much change since the ordinance was passed. For several months Charlene stepped in as President injecting us once again into a busy period of arranging meetings, writing newsletters, and constant telephone conversations. But we both believed we should try to broaden our work for animals rather than spend most of our time on an organization in a county where we didn't even live. With a sense of some relief, she passed the baton to another society president and began searching for new ways to work for animals.

Animal Issues

Without taking a census of my vegetarian friends, it seems to me most vegetarians follow their lifestyle for the animals and for their personal health. I gather this from the way my friends talk—they have lots to say on both subjects. I lump animals and the environment together as I consider these motives, feeling animal life — including human life — is at the core of all interest in the environment. Some vegetarians, like my wife, are foresquare firstly for the animals and secondarily happily aware and accepting of the health benefits. Others, like me, originally made the change primarily because of personal health reasons, even though they may have long histories of participation in animal protection activities. I venture to say that only a small number are vegetarians for health reasons with no concern for the animals or vice versa. Those two common reasons behind American vegetarian life are so compelling, most of us have been spurred on by both.

I have not ignored religious and spiritual reasons as I divide motivations up into only two primary parts. Certainly religion promotes more vegetarian practice worldwide than any other cause. I just happen to believe that when a religion teaches its followers not to eat meat, it, rather than the individual believer, has made the decision for the animals. I think this is so whether the idea is to protect God's creation or to promote nonviolence. Violence in the provision of food is not found in taking plant life, only in taking animal life. It is a practical impossibility to take animal lives for food in a nonviolent way. Even religions condoning meat eating have taught compassion and respect for all life. That their modern nonveg followers eat as a result of inhumane, intensive animal confinement and terrifying, horrific slaughterhouse operations is conveniently overlooked by most of their clergy and the followers themselves.

One of my favorite vegetarians, Chuck, is an extremely successful businessman in the paper recycling business. Born into a poor rural Kentucky family, it would have been hard to predict the future interests, activities, and successes of this creative genius. He describes his decision to become a vegetarian as a spiritual one. I thought his use of the word "spiritual" meant religious the first time he told me that, but he went on to explain it this way: "Les, I knew the pain and fear of an animal about to be killed for food. They scream and try to escape and even try to fight back. What must be happening to their spirits?" Good question, I thought. Chuck goes on to tell his own theory that those animal spirits leaving life in such an ugly, terrified, and combative way are absorbed into our spirits if we eat them. Do any of us need to feed our own spirits with such terrible emotions, flowing into our bodies daily from the food we eat? Sounds a little Buddhist, doesn't it, but Chuck is not a Buddhist. He is more right brained than I am, but he got right through to me when he told me about his spiritual motives. He has caused me to wonder if we are vegetarians because we are nonviolent — or are we nonviolent because we are vegetarians — or both?

The environmental vegetarian will argue with clearing forests for beef grazing land and ruining our streams and rivers with runoff of animal waste from feedlots and from chemicals spread on croplands growing animal feed. He points to the fossil fuels gobbled up by our meat farming system and the food distribution supporting it. Each of these is an environmental disaster in need of curtailment before we witness catastrophic ecological collapse on our fragile planet. Not much of an animal argument for vegetarians here so far, I admit, but look at how environmentalists measure the health of our system of life on earth — the rate of species extinction.

Numbers seem to be different every time the species extinction is discussed because no one knows an accurate way to count all the species. Regardless of the actual numbers used to back up their theories, everyone seems to agree that species are disappearing at an alarming rate and, even more worrisome, the rate of disappearance itself is increasing at an alarming rate.

When I was in grade school in the 1940's we discussed the extinction of animals. It was a curiosity to the kids in my class because the loss of an animal species was a very unusual event. We were taught about the dinosaurs and how they had all disappeared at about the same time, but that was ancient history. The only other example we talked about was the Dodo bird, and it was ever so much more interesting than the dinosaurs. Why? Because the Dodo bird became extinct relatively recently during the 1600's — hardly a full step back into recorded history.

Well known world explorers saw the Dodo and wrote about it in their ships' logs. I think we were told that a taxidermist's stuffed example exists somewhere. In my childhood dictionary a pen and ink drawing of the Dodo showed me what he looked like — a portly, bulbous thing with sturdy feet, similar to and about as ugly as a turkey. I'm pretty sure he was flightless. I imagine he was hunted to extinction. Interesting in his own right, the Dodo captured the imaginations of my classmates and me because he was a rare example of extinction in our time. He had been seen and hunted an eaten and written about by people only a few generations ago. He had been here, running around and squawking (no one told me but somehow I know he didn't have a melodious song) and eating and excreting and procreating, and someone or something had killed the last one, and there would never be another Dodo bird in the history of the universe! Heavy stuff for a gradeschooler.

The Dodo made species extinction real to me, although he was the only recent example my teacher offered. There weren't many to choose from in the 1940's. I later learned about the Passenger Pigeon's extinction in the early years of this century, and I had the same feeling —this was an oddity, a rare and momentous event. When I was in grade school no one talked about how many more species were lost this year than five years ago. The extinction numbers game had not begun. Today the kids in grade school still must react to the loss of a species with horror and shock and wonder at the shame of it, but they only do so the first few times they hear of it. Now an environmental buzzword, species extinction assaults the minds of our young so often they have to become desensitized, as perhaps we all must.

I suppose the last example of a species doesn't sense its death means eternity not only for itself as an individual, but for all those like him who who went before. I also suppose the last human would be aware of the enormity of his death, and this is one of the few real differences between human animals and the other animals. But with or without such an awareness in the minds of the last examples of each dying species, such milestones in the history of life on earth haunt us. John Donne commented on the interrelatedness of all men when he said "every man's death diminishes me," but today we begin to sense how all life is connected as we lose irretrievably one kind of life after another, and we begin to know the threat to ourselves and our planet grows as plants and animals disappear.

I think an environmental vegetarian is a vegetarian because of the animals, whether he knows it or not.

Hunting Bambi

Would meat eaters eat meat if they had to kill it themselves? Once a vegetarian you are somehow more aware of the horrors of the slaughterhouse — whether or not you've ever visited one — than you were when your diet contributed to the need for slaughter. It is ironic to think we vegetarians spend our lives bothered by the pain and suffering now caused by the feeding habits of others, but it's true we do. Meateaters find it too easy to train their minds to avoid thinking of meat as part of a formerly living being killed violently for them. Most people in western society have blithely excused themselves from such troubling thoughts. There is, unfortunately, a small vocal group of nonvegs who talk at length about all meat raising cruelties.

I'm speaking, of course, of the hunters who use the horrors of commercial farming and killing meat to justify their own killing. They are the one group who would go right on eating meat even if they had to kill it. Their arguments in favor of hunting are enough to make a vegetarian laugh if he isn't first made sick by the cruel and twisted logic. "I kill my own meat, swiftly and cleanly, and I only kill what I eat," goes the diatribe. "Do you think the way they kill cows and pigs for the supermarket is humane compared with what we do?" hunters ask. Even if we stretch to accept the implied truth in this last question, the greater wrong of the abattoir hardly justifies what the hunter is doing. I think it analogous to a murderer, even a serial killer, trying to excuse his own actions by pointing to the number of people governments kill in wars. A greater wrong can't justify a lesser wrong.

But I think hunting is not even a lesser wrong. Even in the eyes of a vegetarian, there is something more civilized about buying meat at a store than there is about going out and killing it for yourself, especially when all the meat anyone could ever expect to eat is already prepared for cooking and available at a lower cost.

No, I'm certainly not defending buying meat, nor do I believe that breeding animals for food or hiding their slaughter relieve the meateater of his share of responsibility. I am merely trying to show that the hunter's "swift and clean" killing displays to most of us a barbarism that sets him apart from the rest of us, vegs and nonvegs alike. I didn't come to my feelings about hunting quietly musing in my study; I got more than a bellyful of their macho, good-old-boy actions and attitudes living in rural southeastern Indiana.

Our place is 125 acres of rugged wooded hills, cleared on their tops for hayfields, overlooking the Ohio River near a village of 200 people. Most of the county is hilly woods punctuated by open fields, and water is everywhere in streams and farmers' ponds and in the Ohio itself. Such conditions are ideal for deer, and indeed some locals proudly claim our county has more deer per wooded acre than any other county in the U.S. I have never hunted so it was natural we would plan from the beginning that our rural property would not be available to those camouflaged autumnal guerrillas who prowl through the early morning darkness and celebrate sunrise on the day deer season opens with a volley of gunfire more aggressive and frightening than anything the British and the Minutemen did at Lexington and Concord.

Only days after taking possession of our old farmhouse, one of the wealthy owners of a large factory about 20 miles away stopped his new Blazer and knocked on our door, decked out in Abercrombie and Fitch's finest. He had seen a doe bedded down on our property near the highway and was asking permission to go in and claim the prize. Rather politely, we told him we don't want hunting on our land, and just as politely, he left without incident. That was the first time we invoked our no hunting policy.

A month or two later I witnessed a touching adventure which ended at the same spot our rich hunter had seen the doe. Years later I wrote about it in my local newspaper column:

Two Crossings

The Ohio River is half a mile wide and 70 feet deep in front of our home, and there is usually something to see in the river if you park long enough on our front porch. On a chilly December day soon after we began spending our weekends by the river, a strange looking "log" seemed to be floating near the far shoreline. In the late winter and early spring, the river is full of snags—trees, bushes, lumber, or nearly anything that will float. This day was too early for driftwood, and, as I watched the lone "log," I was sure it was moving slowly crosswise rather than downstream with the current.

A half mile swim would tax all but the best swimmers among us. I recall that was my distance record as a Boy Scout, but it was a once in a lifetime event for me. And now in front of my surprised eyes something was swimming through the cold waters, gradually getting farther and farther from the safety of the Kentucky shoreline. Before it had reached the middle of the river the log began to look like the head of a large dog, and finally I could clearly see a deer's head poking out above the river surface. Fascinated, I watched the entire crossing.

As it reached the shallows less than 100 yards from my vantage point, the doe found her footing in the soft mud of the river bottom, haltingly erected herself on slender legs, moved to solid ground, shook off gallons of the river, and calmly walked across the narrow field into a fringe of trees separating the bottom from the highway. Then for a few minutes I couldn't see her at all.

I continued to watch, expecting her to cross the highway and move into the wooded hills near our house. Deer in these parts are so common that spotting one often evokes no comment at all, but this one — this aquatic athlete — was special to me by this time, and I wanted to see her reach the safety of the woods and hills. I imagined she was standing in the trees near the road shivering as she shook and tried to dry out while waiting for the right moment to cross the road. A car approached from the south — not speeding but destined to pass within 20 feet of her hiding place. There was nothing I could do to shoo the deer or warn the driver.

When the car was still 50 feet from the deer, she jumped out and bolted across the road. Fright flashed through my body, but the alert driver saw it in time and stood on his brakes. Probably everyone and everything in the car was shaken up as the brake lights flashed on, the nose of the car scooped down, and the rear end jerked upward. I heard the tires screech as I saw the deer just clear the front of the car and bound off into the woods unhurt. The car and its occupants recovered, started up, and drove on out of sight.

Each year some 400 million animals are killed on our roads. Also 120 people are killed in collisions with animals, 8000 are injured, and an estimated $40 million in property damage is sustained by vehicles. Most of us feel badly if we hit a bird or a squirrel, but if we become involved in an accident with a deer or a cow or a horse, real danger to ourselves and loss of property are added to our pangs of sympathy for the animal. Beyond being vigilant and watching our speed, small ultrasonic whistles are available to attach to a car's front bumpers. These alert devices, used by some state patrols, will scare animals away from the road reducing the chance of collisions.

My friend the swimming doe was lucky that day, and I imagine she wondered why crossing 20 feet of highway was so much more dangerous than crossing a half mile of river.

Thinking back over those two incidents it now occurs to me the doe on the hill and the doe who swam the river to get to that hill were likely one and the same. I can't be certain, but I prefer to think they were. Our refusal to let her be killed gave her more life and adventure including swimming the river both ways. That's the sort of thing she was put on this earth for, not to be rendered into a few frozen packs of tough, wild tasting meat waiting for our mid-American manufacturing person to call in his friends for a feast.

Actually the man who asked our permission and left politely once it was denied is the most exemplary type of hunter. (I cringe to think it's really possible to use the terms "exemplary" and "hunter" in the same sentence.) The more numerous ones troubling me the most are those who don't ask and do their violence on your land anyway. They know you can't police over 100 acres of hills and woods effectively. Posted with no hunting signs or not, they freely cross border fences intent on murdering the same beautiful creatures I try to make welcome with salt licks. Until the shooting starts, you don't know they're around, and when it does, you're still not sure if they're on your land or a neighbor's. To make matters worse, you're afraid to walk into your own woods to find out — afraid some yo-yo will take a pot shot at something big he can't see well coming down the side of a hill toward him.

If you're foolish enough to walk your woods during hunting season, hope all the poachers get on and get off your land without your noticing them. An undereducated good old boy hating the guts of city slickers who come down here, buy up the land, and then try to keep the natives off it won't be happy to see you if you do run across him out there hunting in your woods. You represent right (he knows he's wrong), power and the law (he knows you can file a complaint against him), and trouble (in the form of fines and jail if your complaint sticks). In a community where everyone knows everyone else, if he's seen, he's identified. You have just walked into a most uncomfortable confrontation.

Now he's standing there armed and you're just standing there. This is where you hope the Baptist Sunday schools in the local area have really done their job. If they have, he can act lost and ask if he's still on the tract next door, or he can tell you he wounded an animal and has been following him for a quarter mile to put him out of his misery. It's unlikely, but he can acknowledge his error, apologize, and leave. Or he can make you into the victim of one of those hunting accidents we read about. Considering the possibilities, you stay out of the woods in deer season.

Hunters have some really great answers to the charge they have all the weapons while the animals have none, so where's the sport? In this vegetarian's view, their reactions to this idea only make matters worse. "Not sporty enough for you, well I hunt with a muzzleloader." (Here you may substitute "bow and arrow," if you like.) Now that makes lots of sense to an animal protectionist. Who do these guys think they are, golfers with handicaps? Are the muzzleloaders saying, "I'm so good I use something that doesn't shoot straight and can't be fired in rapid succession, and I also burden myself with powder horns and caps or flints, and I can still put those wily devils on my plate?" Is the bowhunter saying, "I have to get right on top of a deer to get a shot at him; that spots him a hundred yards or so to be sure it's sporty?" Handicaps my clavicle, these guys are to hunting what Lizzy Borden is to Lee Harvey Oswald — no less murderers, just cruder.

From the deer's point of view, I suspect he'd rather be shot by a modern deer gun any day than any cruder weapon, especially a bow and arrow. Adrian Benke, a bowhunter himself, wrote *The Bowhunting Alternative*, a great little book telling you everything that's wrong with bowhunting. Compared to a hunter with a modern gun, a bowhunter can't hit the broad side of a barn. If he hits an animal, he probably wont hit a vital organ as with a gun. Instead the arrow will slice the animal open, leaving him free to run away and bleed to death slowly.

I had a bow and arrow set when I was a kid. The big circular target was stuffed with straw and stored in our garage attic between uses until a family of mice nested in it and we threw it away. The arrows had little metal points like bullets, and Mom and Dad lectured me endlessly about only shooting at the target. Years later I thought that was the kind of arrow a bowhunter uses — I was really naive.

Walking through my woods, I found a lost hunter's arrow recently. It didn't look anything like my childhood target arrows. The business end looked like the feathers on the old target arrow, except, instead of being made out of feathers, it was made out of stainless steel razor blades. I was shocked at the lethal pattern of four triangular scalpels, each about three inches long and three quarters inch wide at its widest point. So that's what Adrian Benke called a broadhead. No matter where it hit, it could let enough blood out of a mastodon to kill it slowly. Most of us nonhunting city slickers just don't have any idea what bowhunting is all about.

The bows these modern Robin Hoods use don't look anything like my old, slightly warped, target bow either. Tonto never saw a modern compound hunting bow with its system of pulleys, flexible member of space age materials, and sights with micrometer adjustments. An archer in the Crusades wouldn't have known what to do with one of these things.

Outfitted with all this sophistication, the bowhunter can come on to your posted property, stalk his prey, wound or kill it, and leave without any more sound than the dripping of blood pumping out of the haunch of his terrified victim. You can be in your house two hundred yards away and never know he was there.

More on Hunting

I can't imagine a vegetarian hunter, but I suppose there must be one somewhere. I've tried to guess what sort of person he would be, but I just can't get a mental picture of such a rare bird. Would he be a compassionate person because he avoids eating animals? Can anyone decry and boycott intensive animal farming and inhumane slaughter and still look down the sights of a gun and blow some woodland creature away? The more I try to imagine such a hunter, the less likely I think he exists. A vegetarian hunter is an oxymoron.

Still, not every hunter hunts for food; consider the trophy hunters. I never thought a lot about trophies until I became active in animal protection work about five years ago, but I remember a couple of trophies that touched my early life. One was a moose and the other a deer.

I palled around with Tom for several years starting at age eleven when our family moved into his neighborhood. Tom's dad was a hunter and proud of it. My dad wasn't, but didn't militate against it, so I didn't have too many thoughts about hunting in those years. A couple of deer heads hung on the walls in Tom's house. I suppose they were great works of taxidermy, if you appreciate such things. One was large and erect and its neck gracefully curved so his regal, antlered head looked off at an angle to the left. After some early curiosity, I tended to ignore the deer when I was at Tom's house.

Tom's house had a small den, his dad's domain, with a leather chair, bookcases, and a desk. We always went through the den when we went from his back door, our usual entrance, to the front hall stairs and on up to his room to play. One day as we cut through the den,

I was transfixed by the largest, blackest animal I had ever seen. Actually it was only part of an animal, the head and neck of a moose. Tom's dad had been to Canada, and this thing is what he brought back with him. Horses and cows have big heads when you get up close to them, but a moose's head is something else again - more like the front end of a steam locomotive sticking a yard and a half into the room.

You really had to walk around the moose to get through the den. It wasn't just a decoration — it was to the room what a car is to its garage. The heavy, paddle-like antlers reached up to touch the eight foot ceiling, forcing the mass of the head and neck to be mounted so low on the wall that even as an eleven year old, I could stare straight into his black glass eyes. I remember running my fingers through his long coarse fur, but it didn't feel good like petting my dog — it was somehow just there.

One thing the moose had I had never seen before was a wattle, a fur covered appendage about the size of a blackjack, hanging from the bottom of his horizontal neck. It was swivelly attached to the neck, and none of us kids could resist the temptation to grab it like it was a rope to a train whistle and say, "toot toot," each time we ran through the den. Tom got in the most trouble when the wattle eventually detached from the neck requiring the services of a taxidermist to put it back on. Thereafter, on pain of unspeakable punishments, we abandoned the toot toot business.

The other trophy I remember well was Elmer the deer. He belonged to my dad, who hadn't killed him. I think Elmer had been found at a flea market, and for a dollar or two, Dad brought him home to mount in our garage to entertain my sister and me. Elmer, who must have been mounted in the 1920's was already old and in poor condition, looking sort of moth-eaten, when we got him — certainly not comparable to the expensive trophies at Tom's house. My sister Jean and I named Elmer, and we liked him. He had beautiful brown eyes, and his modest rack of horns was still in good condition.

Our garage in those days was two cars long and one car wide with a steep pitched roof and widely spaced rafters so you could look up into the attic space. At the end nearest the house rose a plastered wall all the way up to the point of the roof. Dad mounted Elmer up there looking out over our old Packard and Chrysler sleeping nose to tail in the garage below. On weekends, the cars sunned outside in the driveway, and Dad was in the garage with his woodworking tools. We hung around, mindful of our friend Elmer up there watching us.

Mom hated Elmer, not because she hated hunting—I doubt if she ever thought much about it—but because he was dirty. She was pretty fastidious, and she couldn't be happy with that old partial carcass, even stuck way up there in the garage. For all she knew, it could have bugs in it. Periodically she proposed to get rid of it, but Jean and I resisted throughout our younger years. In my first year of college while I wasn't around, Mom got Dad to climb up into the garage attic, unhook Elmer from the spike that held him up there all those years, blow the dust off him, and donate him to an auction to raise money for some new community tennis courts.

The evening of the auction, I was home from school, so I dropped by to join our neighbors gathered on the spreading lawn of one of the larger homes in the area. The donations looked like a rummage sale—old furniture, knickknacks, skis, wagons, scooters, a dog house, and, much to my surprise piled on top of someone else's rummage, Elmer, looking straight up into the sky. I knew then my mother had a treacherous, secretive side I'd never seen before, but I also had to admit I was getting a little old for Elmer, no matter how I had loved him in earlier years.

The auction began slowly with the men and women bidding cautiously for items in the huge pile. I had no place to sit in my almost white slacks, so I acquired a chair for fifty cents high bid and sat down in it to the amusement of the crowd. Elmer was one of the early items, and bidding started at ten cents with interest slacking off as the high bid reached sixty cents. I couldn't help myself when, just before the hammer fell to Mom's horror, I said, "seventy-five cents," and the auctioneer said, "SOLD" before anyone else had a chance to bid.

The organizer of the event then stood up and urged the crowd to loosen up and bid more for the items. This was, after all, a fund raiser. The crowd was swept up in the spirit of the event, and soon even opening bids on anything were well beyond my meager college boy's pocketbook. They raised lots of money that night; I donated the chair back and it sold for twenty dollars, and I loaded Elmer in the car and took him home.

Mom won in the long run, and I'm not even sure what happened to Elmer. My guess is he was laid to rest in the town dump. Now as I look back on the few trophies in my life, I realize I disliked the moose because he clearly didn't belong in a house, and I loved Elmer just because I had him so long. But these were childhood attitudes — I wouldn't be caught dead with a trophy in my house now. (caught dead?) Every time I see a trophy now, I know the taxidermist has not worked to show reality. Instead he has tried to create beauty by restoring the natural form to the beheaded front end of a once free spirit who died terrified, lying on the ground, torn apart and spurting blood while diminishing spasms jerked his body and his useless legs still twitched as he tried to run. If the taxidermist wants to depict reality, he should make the trophies gruesome.

In 1989, the sick-minded Bison hunts conducted by Montana's government just outside Yellowstone National Park prompted the following in my weekly newspaper column:

The Sport of Buffalo Hunting

There was a time when much of America was the home of the buffalo, but as civilization exploded westward across this continent in the last century, the numbers and habitat of the American Buffalo shrank to near obscurity.

Today the buffalo in Yellowstone Park are a peaceful bunch — the National Park Service does not allow them to be hunted, and they aren't afraid of people. Sadly, last year when fires destroyed large areas of the park, many of the park's buffalo were started down a road to their destruction at the hands of trophy hunters.

In the months following the fire, buffalo herds had to range further from their traditional grazing areas to find enough to eat. The park is a vast area, and its borders are not fenced, so many left the park as they foraged for food. For the Montana Fish, Wildlife and Parks Department the stage was now set for them to throw a party for their patrons, the hunters, who pay their license fees to Montana.

For the price of a permit, the Montana authorities acted as guides for groups of "hunters" (but I think "shooters" is a better word here because no one had to hunt for the buffalo). These happy little parties were escorted within point blank range of the lazy, grazing, totally tame herds of park buffalo sometimes less than $1/4$ mile outside the park boundary. Clearly these sportsmen not only didn't have to hunt, the didn't have to be marksmen either. Each macho woodsman could step right up and shoot him a buffalo. It was the equivalent of shooting ducks in a mill pond.

Unfortunately, a 2000 pound buffalo can't be killed with a single shot, and most kept moving, although slower and slower as more lead was pumped into them. Once down they tried repeatedly to get up as still more shots were fired — execution style. One poor animal tried to stand up 41 times! Shooters interviewed at the site were pleased to get their trophies and grinningly said they'd do it again if they had the chance.

This grisly little story is a reminder that many agencies and organizations with "conservation," "wildlife," or "natural resources" in their names are really pro-hunting.

The National Park Service believes the animals should not be given supplemental food apparently taking the position that nature will work out the proper solution. A similar line of thought guided their policy against fighting forest fires which led to the blackening of much of Yellowstone. But you can't mess with Mother Nature some of the time and leave her to her devices other times. If these animals had not been relegated to the status of tame zoo animals within the park's protection, perhaps they would have retained enough natural fear of man to make these killing parties less successful.

We can thank the Fund for Animals (200 West 57th Street, NY, NY 10019) for the details of these sordid bloodlettings; they had an observer in one of the parties shooting with a video camera, and they have implored the National Park Service to feed the buffalo and the Montana authorities to stop the shoots. They have appeared before Congress on behalf of the buffalo, but still the killing goes on.

If you are moved to help, the Fund for Animals depends on donations and can provide much informative material on hunting. Any amount will help in their work. Also you can write to the Director, National Parks Service, Department of the Interior, Washington DC 20013 and ask them to feed the buffalo to keep them inside the park.

The Cuvier Press Club

Among the meat eating memories of this vegetarian are a tangle of thoughts of the old Cuvier Press Club on Garfield Place in Cincinnati. In the late 1960's and early 1970's when I visited there and was briefly a member, it was primarily a downtown men's lunch club. They had a range of other functions including a number of social events, but by far the most patronized activities of the club were its bar and its lunches. In my time the club had no connection with the press despite its name. Upon nomination and approval, anyone who could pay dues, eat meat, and drink liquor could join.

The Cuvier sat on the north side of Garfield Place in the block west of the Cincinnati library. You might call it a small mansion or a large old home; its stone block walls and huge front windows were set back only a few feet from the sidewalk. Inside, high ceilings and dark finished old woodwork suggested its early service as the home of a wealthy Cincinnati family. The building still exists as the city's Butterworth Senior Citizens Center. In the downstairs areas (I can't remember being upstairs), by far the most prominent feature was the bar paralleling the long side of the largest room. Tables for four filled the rest of the room. The next room had a window looking to the street and a long table where the same members gathered every day for the noonday meal. The kitchen area was hidden from the drinkers and diners receiving and disgorging busy waiters through swinging doors. At lunch the old Cuvier throbbed with people, and late comers sometimes waited at the bar if a stool was available.

To a meat eater, the Cuvier's cooking was reason to celebrate. The menu listed a variety of meat and fish dishes and always a special.

Braised lamb shanks, I'm now somewhat embarrassed to say, were one of my favorite specials. My friend, Joe, and I drove from the outskirts of town at least twice a week just to enjoy lunch in those old rooms. We came mostly to eat, but others came mostly to drink.

Joe had become a member of the Cuvier on a special deal designed to attract new members; he was admitted for half the annual dues of $125. I thought that was a bargain after several lunches there as Joe's guest, so I asked if I could get in on a similar deal. Although the special arrangement had expired, Joe said he'd see what he could do and later told me I was all set. I handed in my check for $62.50 and began attending as a member. It became obvious something had gone wrong when, six months later, I was billed for dues again. I had been let in for only six months. Thinking it over, I realized that nearly every time I used the club, Joe was along, so I didn't need to be a member. I decided not to renew, ending my status as a member but not as a frequenter.

Joe had his own problems with the cost of belonging to the club. His special deal had indeed given him a full year of membership, but his troubles were bigger than my little $62.50 dispute. A designer by trade, Joe had done some work for the club, probably having to do with redecorating. He sent his bill for $300, but it was never paid. Not one to harass anyone about an overdue bill, Joe waited as long as he could and then inquired of the club manager. There was some discussion and confusion, and finally he was told the club thought he had donated his services. The matter came to a standstill, and the bill remained unpaid. In frustration, Joe told the club he would take his $300 out in annual dues. While continuing to presume the privileges of membership, he stopped paying dues for about two and a half years.

My guess is the guys who handled the dues and the payables were the same ones who arrived every day about 10:00 A.M. and kept the bartender busy until they weaved their way out of the club at 4:00 P.M. They were all older sales types who worked their repertoire of stories gathered over a lifetime on each other or on anyone willing to bend an elbow with them. Joe and I used to imagine their copious, overflowing posteriors had permanent round impressions the size of the seats on the Cuvier's barstools.

The biggest social event of the year at the Cuvier was Wild Game Night. Tickets cost $25.00 each, an exorbitant price then, and anyone could buy a ticket, member or not. I attended several. Some of the club members were hunters, and they supplied much of the food from their freezers. Favorite recipes for each exotic meat were done proud by the Cuvier's excellent chefs. Having gone on for years, the February event was always a crowded sellout.

On arriving at Wild Game Night, a table full of ice covered with oysters on the half shell greeted the revellers. Dinner was served from a buffet line full of strange looking dishes identified with typed place cards. I never before or since had some of the "delicacies" I had at Wild Game Night. I can recall roast bear and buffalo and wild turkey and rattlesnake meat. Some of the smaller furry forest animals were cooked as well, but by now my vegetarian brain has begun to block out memories of them. Most celebrants took only small portions of the wild meats, not always liking their special flavors. I recall liking buffalo well enough to have seconds, but most of the other dishes were only curiosities to me.

The Cuvier sold the building in the 1970's, operated for a few years from a rented top floor dining room in one of Cincinnati's old skyscrapers, and finally bit the dust as patronage dwindled away. Toward the end, anyone, member or not, could have lunch there, but they still couldn't attract enough business to stay open. By the time it closed I had not eaten there in a couple of years. Thinking back to its heyday and the Wild Game Nights from my vegetarian viewpoint, they never offered anything I could eat today. And while I must patronize many a restaurant preparing beef, pork, chicken, etc., I purposely avoid those offering exotic wild animal foods. Maybe if I had been a vegetarian back in the Wild Game Night times, I'd have been outside carrying a sign objecting to hunting instead of inside eating wild animals. Having said that, I ask myself if cooking beef and pork is any less reprehensible than cooking buffalo and wild turkey. Knowing the cruelties of both meat farming and hunting, I wouldn't care to argue either side of that issue.

Michael Klaper said it best: "I don't eat anything that ever had a face, a mother and father, or that runs from me when I'm thinking about having it for lunch."

This Lacto-Ovo Thing

I have a tee shirt sporting a Greg Larson "Far Side" cartoon showing cave men toting a huge carrot to their cave. The caption reads, "Early vegetarians home from the hunt." Great humor in the best Larson tradition, but of course it has nothing to do with what early vegetarians were really like.

Certainly the farther back in time you go, the more likely a vegetarian followed his lifestyle because of his religious beliefs. Only a few decades ago, the health motivations for a vegetarian diet were unknown or at best only guesses. Whatever form religious teachings about animals took, they usually boiled down to protecting God's creations or avoiding causing suffering to animals. How better to do that than not to kill them for food? Even in religions condoning eating meat, there is a fuzzy concept of humane slaughter. Today, for the pitifully little good it does, we have also a federal humane slaughter law in the U.S.

But how much reflection is required to bring the idea of humane slaughter into question? Isn't this the mother of all contradictions in terms? Short of euthanizing some sleeping animal with a lethal injection of a barbiturate, can slaughter, by any honest person's thinking, be humane? I think not and so must have countless other vegetarians farther back in time than history can record. The simplest answer to the impossibility of humane slaughter is not to eat the flesh of animals. Milk and eggs are quite another matter.

I won't argue here the morality of using animals to help in the work of people. Oxen pulling carts, horses carrying riders, dogs tending sheep, and sheep providing wool are all, at first glance, not necessarily inhumane uses of animals. I say, "not necessarily" with some emphasis because it is quite possible, even likely, to find abuse of those working animals, but their work could be done without such abuse. Into this same broad category of acceptable use, early vegetarians must have placed taking eggs from a chicken's nest and milk from the lactating cow.

It's sad to say that in our modern, dollar efficient world little care is given to avoid the abuse of those animals who work for man. In too many cases, abuse is deliberately selected to cut costs. This lack of concern for the animal gives credence to those champions of animals who call for ending all use of animals by man. But certainly in the world of the early vegetarian, few if any would have objected to riding on the back of a horse, using the wool of a sheep, drinking the milk of a cow, or eating the egg of a chicken. One could be a lacto-ovo vegetarian and believe he was doing his part to prevent the abuse and suffering of animals. Today we are neither so innocent nor so lucky.

All large scale production in the United States is guided by dollar efficiency. This applies to automobiles and cheese, washing machines and eggs. Dollar efficiency is an inescapable discipline all industry must adopt or die. Dollar return must be maximized.

In the presence of such a pervasive discipline, every abuse of animals in our food production system is devised and perpetuated or allowed to happen because the producer believes money will be saved over less abusive alternatives. The unyielding law we blindly obey requiring us to maximize dollar returns *in each and every instance of food animal abuse* obliterates our humane and spiritual beliefs about the protection of God's creatures. Dollar efficiency causes lifetimes of hell and hoary, terrifying, sometimes prolonged and tortured deaths to six billion animals every year. Not the least of these abuses attend the dairy and egg industries.

As I said before, the early vegetarian was luckier than we are — he could eat his eggs and cheese and drink his milk and cream without pangs of conscience — acts hardly possible now. Lacto and ovo vegetarians were true to their convictions about animal abuse. Even a few decades ago as we began to organize bits and pieces of knowledge about nutrition, the case for lacto-ovo vegetarian eating seemed to be strengthening. You could be sure of getting plenty of protein and all of your essential amino aids and B-12 from these animal foods according to the wisdom of the times. Here was a way to follow your heart an protect your health without giving up too much from your old nonveg days.

Now we know that total vegetarians get all the protein they need and synthesize all the essential amino acids They can emphasize B-12 in their diets or supplement with pills. As our knowledge of nutrition expanded, the health reasons earlier suggested for vegetarians eating dairy and eggs disappeared. In the same time interval, the practices of humane dairy and egg production also disappeared.

There are still the occasional family farms producing dairy products and eggs while handling their animals in a humane fashion, but the preponderance of producers are cruel factory farms maximizing dollar returns and subjecting their animals to lives of constant horror. I can only believe the humane motivations once prompting lacto-ovo vegetarians are no longer appropriate, and using dairy and egg products is now no different than eating meat in its animal suffering consequences.

I used to enjoy cheese on almost anything—my hamburgers, my vegetables, my apple pie, even my eggs—you name it and I have tried it and usually liked it with cheese. Brie at a cocktail party, mozzarella on a pizza, cottage cheese, Roquefort and even limburger were favorites. I don't think I ever met a cheese I didn't like. Milk was another passion long after those early years when bottle babies such as I needed it for calcium. As an adult in my forties and early fifties, I fooled myself into thinking a glass of that stuff before bed helped me to sleep. (I eventually discovered it was the problem, not the solution, but the old habit died hard and I always wanted milk at bedtime.)

Eggs were another favorite of mine in my preveg days. As with cheese, I never met an egg dish I didn't like. The toughest decision in the morning was fried over or sunny side up, scrambled, poached, soft boiled, or hard boiled. And while I agonized over those choices, it really didn't matter — I always thought they were great when they were served. I ate them with nearly any seasoning except ketchup, including butter, salt, pepper, seasoned salt, onion chips, Hollandaise, Worcestershire sauce, and cheese. Although in recent writings I've referred to eggs as oval shaped capsules of death through coronary artery disease, I confess to being an egg addict earlier in life.

One breakfast I learned to love, biscuits and gravy with a pair of eggs sunny side up, did not come from my Mom's farm roots. In fact, I can't remember her ever fixing it for me. My overindulgence in that dish developed much more recently from life at our retreat in rural Indiana. The only breakfasts you could get at the local cafes were the simple ones—eggs, bacon toast, fried potatoes, and biscuits and gravy. I took to this morning monstrosity the way a beagle chases a rabbit. Every time we went out for breakfast in Indiana in my preveg days, I ate eggs and biscuits and gravy. With all that cholesterol and saturated fat combined with my propensity for accumulating too many blood lipids, it's a wonder my circulatory system didn't become so viscous with sludge that the blood stopped running around my body altogether.

Becoming a vegetarian wasn't as tough as I thought it would be. If I had decided to be a lacto-ovo vegetarian, it would have been even easier, but it would have made a much smaller improvement in my health, and it would have left me with an inescapable guilt for the concomitant suffering of the dairy cows, the veal calves, the debeaked chickens in battery cages, and the bags of baby chicks thrown away at birth to suffocate under the weight of their brothers.

SECTION SIX

ENVIRONMENT

Rainy Days

Thirty years ago, Dad retired and he and Mom left the Chicago area for a new home on the west coast of Florida. In the years leading up to retirement they had taken their vacations at a small fishing resort on Lemon Bay near the town of Englewood. Dad loved fishing like I loved Mom's cooking, but I knew at an early age I wasn't patient enough to make a good fisherman. At age sixty-two, Dad looked forward to spending lots of time with his boat and rod and reel out in the bay and in the Gulf of Mexico. Mom was often along for the fun.

I had never been to Florida when they moved there, but I always wanted to go. I remember in college envying the kids who ran off to Florida during spring break, but I always had something else to do. My first trip, then, was to visit Mom and Dad and to see their new home. I hated winters, yet I had always lived up north. I was fascinated with palm trees, probably just because we couldn't have them where I grew up in Illinois and Ohio. I bounced up the steps to a Delta flight to Tampa with a sense of high adventure eager for the discoveries awaiting me.

Their retirement home was idyllic. The broad lawn terminated at a sea wall to keep Lemon Bay at bay. A mangrove island in front of the home cackled with nesting pelicans and egrets. Dad's boat swung slightly within the limits of its lines in a boat basin cut into the yard. On around the shoreline of their little cove was a large old wooden fishing boat with blue paint peeling off its cabin. Two palms curved out over the sea wall completing a scene an artist would dream up.

Dad and Mom were happy, proud hosts, and we all explored the area together seeing Venice and Boca Grande and Sarasota. In the boat we cruised around the many islands in Lemon Bay, beached the craft at

Stump Pass for picnics and, one cold morning at an extra low tide, put on some old galoshes and went slogging through mud flats to discover huge colonies of clams buried in the muck. Of course Mom cooked clams for us that evening. This was the first of dozens of trips to Florida that ended only when I finally retired and moved there myself.

In late spring I returned to Florida for another short visit. The weather had turned very warm flushing the snowbirds into flight for their nesting areas in the midwest and points east. Florida was left to non-migratory species like Mom and Dad and the younger people who lived there year round to tend the stores, build the houses, and fix the cars. Now well settled into his new home, Dad busied himself with his garage woodworking tools building shelves and a new set of hurricane shutters for the house. I enjoyed wasting my time reading novels, sitting on the seawall, and rocking the boat in its basin. Morning warmth progressed into midday heat and afternoon oppression. I knew why the snowbirds had flown away.

The sun tried to push everything back like the blaze of a roaring bonfire at a high school pep rally, but the best shelter, short of the air conditioned house was in the shade of the cabbage palms. I peeled off all non-essential clothing and regarded the heat, this new harsh aspect of my long sought wonderland. Dad paced himself carefully in the garage. Looking at the eastern sky I spied a wall of thunderheads towering to heights unfamiliar to a midwesterner. It seemed a hundred thousand witches were furiously boiling their pots in the middle of the state. Overhead the sky was clear.

A light sea breeze came across the yard helping, but not solving the heavy heat. "Is there any rain in those clouds?" I asked Dad. "Oh sure; it'll be here at three o'clock," he said. When I asked how he knew when it would rain, he smiled and told me to wait and see. I returned to my time wasting, now with an eye on the wall of clouds, brilliant white in the afternoon sun. Yes, they were moving my way even in the face of the light breeze from the west.

By two thirty the wall showed itself to have forward and rearward portions. I could see the dark grey bottoms of the clouds, and the rumble of thunder kept drawing my attention away from the book. The sea breeze disappeared leaving an eerie stillness. Did the birds know what was coming? The pelicans and gulls were nowhere to be seen by two forty five. The first puffs of wind smelling of rain swept the yard as if they had been let in through cracks in the invisible canopy of heat. The sky darkened, thunder grew louder, wind asserted itself smartly, and the first round drops of rain dotted the front walk disappearing as the residual heat in the cement drove them back into vapor. Now was the time to duck into the garage. A heavy downpour began as quickly as if someone had turned on a showerhead.

Dad pointed to his watch — it was three o'clock. Up north a line of thunderstorms means a cold front and signals a change in the weather for a few days. As this rain beat down on us, the temperature dropped into the low eighties, and I thought maybe the vacation wouldn't be so hot after all. By three fifteen, the rain dwindled and stopped and the sky brightened. By dinner time the heat had returned correcting my ideas about a cold front. "It's like this every day in the summer, son," Dad told me. "It helps things grow, but it really doesn't kill the heat for long." I came to know this predictable daily afternoon rainstorm had been a feature of Florida's west coast climate since before weather records were kept.

If he could be here today, Dad would be shocked at the climatic change on the gulf coast since those days thirty years ago. We still get the heat in the late spring and summer, and most days that wall of clouds still tantalizes as it slowly moves west. While it often comes close enough so you can hear the thunder, it no longer rains every day. The brief summer pattern showers come perhaps once or twice a week, and their times aren't predictable. When they do come, they occasionally wait until evening. Frontal and tropical storm rains account for a much larger portion of the area's total rainfall now. The annual rainfall and underground water tables reflect this unhappy change in climate, and Florida's west coast — once a water wonderland — now has to restrict water usage as supplies dwindle and population increases.

If you don't live here, you may not know, Florida is a big ranching state. A few miles east of the populated coastal areas where most people live and most others vacation, large tracts of land have been cleared for grazing cattle. In southern Florida, the interior areas have been converted to beef and agriculture steadily over the last several decades. Gone are pine forests, palmetto scrublands, and swampy, steamy areas, and in their places grasslands and croplands have appeared. South Florida's new agricultural heartland can't create the amounts of moisture that used to boil up into thunderheads every day. It's a vegetarian's environmental nightmare. In thirty short years those daily drenchings you could set your watch by have gone and the water they carried to the coast is now trucked to the meat market in the form of sides of beef.

Environment

I live on a barrier island, and the Gulf of Mexico laps at the end of my front yard. Sometimes "laps" is the wrong word as storms and winds whip up waves as tall as a man and drive them on shore to explode against a wall of rocks placed there to keep this fragile strip of land from being washed beneath the surface. I've read about the rock bound coast of Maine, but those rocks are placed there by nature. The rocks binding parts of Florida's coast were set there one by one by tall cranes. Experts agree armoring a beach with a rock revetment will hasten the disappearance of the beach sands, but in some places, the only alternative to placing the rocks would be to lose the houses nearest the water. You can make a good case for not building anything on these constantly changing, snaky strips of land.

Fortunately my house is not so close that the rocks in front of it are essential to its survival, but they are part of a long line of armor protecting some houses very close to the water. The result of these rocks is that our beach has eroded, and at times the water comes right up to the rocks. Happily, during the last year we've seen a reversal of the trend as sand moved landward. Now, especially at low tide, a modest little beach invites barefoot treks north and south picking up shells, watching seabirds, chatting with neighbors, and sniffing the seabreezes.

Most of the life in the sea is invisible to a beachwalker, but bits and pieces show themselves, often after their own lives have ended. Last week low tide presented on our beach a beautiful fish about four feet long and weighing perhaps eighty to one hundred pounds, lying there dead. Not being a fisherman, I guessed it was a tarpon, but I'm still not sure. It had silvery electric blue sides and belly and a dark top. Its jutting lower jaw suggested an underbite, and half dollar sized diamond shaped scales reflected glints of the setting sun. This had been a magnificent animal, the kind proud fishermen hoist up on docks and stand next to for pictures.

No injury was visible on this trophy quality fish; it had died from some illness or perhaps old age. I wondered, though, how many creatures of the sea just got old and died. More likely they are eventually preyed upon by another sea creature or by man. Only the tiniest part of man's threat to a fish like this one on our beach are the sportfishermen's hooks and lines. Far more serious are man's throwaways: chemicals, toxins, and garbage dumped into the once pristine salt water world of fish, turtles, whales, shellfish, and plants.

Within a week the beach below our house yielded up another giant corpse, this time a Loggerhead turtle with a shell three feet long. Although her shell had been crushed, a local expert suggested the injury could have been caused by a boat after it died and floated to the surface. Such a streamlined animal, dead on the beach and drawing flies to land on its bright green flippers, stirred a sad discomfort in all of us as we watched experts examine it and later bury it. The fish's appearance had gone unrecorded, but the turtle's demise made the local newspapers. The Loggerhead is an endangered species, so the count of their dead found on beaches in this county notched up one to a total of ten this year so far. Again I wondered if it could have been old age, but I didn't really believe it. Much more likely and much more perturbing, that turtle was killed by his own poisoned environment.

When you stand on a beach and look out over a 180 degree span of empty water, it makes you feel small. Then look at a map and realize how little of the sea you can really see, and you'll feel infinitesimal. If in one week's time, two giant sea creatures bodies are washed ashore on the small portion of the world's beaches I walk, what is going on out there in the middle of the gulfs and seas and oceans? I'm staggered to think of how much damage we have done and are doing to the waters of the world. What's happening to the environment on dry land and in the atmosphere isn't a happier story, although it may be better known because it can be better seen.

Someone once suggested you could think of the earth as an apple and our biosphere—the land, seas, and atmosphere where all life exists —as the skin on that apple. The earth seems huge, but that thin skin of the earth we live on suddenly seems small once we've run through the apple analogy. In this constricted habitat, man and all the other forms of life must find food, mine materials, produce goods, live, reproduce, dispose of wastes and die. That's a lot of activity by countless organisms in a small space. No wonder the fish and turtles are having trouble — their living space has been used by man as a dumping place, conveniently hiding the evidence. But there is no way to hide the results of man's dirty work when the creatures start washing up on the beech.

I think you don't have to be a vegetarian to care about the environment, but it helps if you are. Automatically a vegetarian is doing something about the environment because he is consuming a much smaller share of the earth's resources than his nonveg counterpart. I've wondered too if vegetarians aren't naturally more disposed to recycle, conserve water and other resources, use more biodegradable products, and create less waste than the animal eaters of the world. I have no way to prove such a notion, but as I think of my vegetarian friends as a group and compare them to my nonveg friends, I sense it may be so. It's hard to define environment except in terms of life, and it's hard to live as a vegetarian without a special reverence for life, and so I carry around the unsupportable but compelling idea that vegetarians are more committed environmentalists than nonvegs. I think we feel a sharper pain as we come upon a dead fish on a beach or a sick cormorant dehydrating on the sunny sand. We feel and understand, perhaps on a deeper level, the connectedness of all life and our personal loss as the turtle dies or the pelicans dwindle from lack of food. How could we go on without the animals? Why would we want to?

※※※

Over a year ago, I wrote the following piece on the environment in my newspaper column. It presents an interesting way to reflect on the environment.

Defining the Environment

We all know the environment is important, and we know it is threatened, but if we were asked to describe the environment or to draw a picture of it, I'm sure most of us would be stumped. It's hard to do that when what you're trying to describe isn't a "thing." I ran across a little progression of words I think can help us in a search for the meaning of environment:

atom

molecule

cell

tissue

organ

organism

ecosystem

Earth

Obviously this is a list of various organizations of matter in progressively more complex order, and from "cell" on through the list, we can associate the quality, life, with each item on the list. Whoever first wrote down this list clearly had life in mind just as I think we must when we consider the meaning of environment. For after all, to define "environment" we need to ask, "environment of what?", and the answer to "what?" is usually something living. The way we use environment today, it has to do with the compatibility of various forms of life with their surroundings. We're not too interested in the environment of a rock on the moon, but we do want to know if life on the moon can exist.

Now to go back to the list, we can see each life form on the list is dependent on the forms above and below it. An organ — like the heart - would die if the tissues it is made of die, and it would just as certainly die if the organism it serves — say a human — were to die. This dependence on the steps above and below is equally true for organisms (plants and animals). Our life as an organism depends upon the vitality of the ecosystem in which we live for it provides the food, shelter, oxygen, energy, etc. we need. We are just as dependent on the ecosystem (the step above) as we are on our organs (the step below).

But the really interesting thing in this progressive list is that an ecosystem — and let's define it as the interaction of all living things in a given area — and even the Earth itself — which is a collection of ecosystems — could be considered forms of life. And if we can accept that idea, then we can begin to grasp the meaning and importance of the concept of "environment." We can understand that humans cannot live on indefinitely regardless of their effects on other living things, or on ecosystems. We can begin to see we must take care to protect not only those ecosystems in which we live, but all ecosystems throughout the world, for even the Earth, as a living thing, can be killed if enough of its component parts are killed.

Some say the environmental movement really got its wings in 1969 when the first pictures of the Earth were taken from space. The perfect blue sphere wrapped in feathery white clouds with small continents peeking through was so much more beautiful than any artist or mapmaker had ever dreamed. Compared to the lifeless piles of rock making up our moon and other planets, this one looked different; it looked alive and hospitable and uniquely attractive — something to cherish and protect.

But even in twenty short years the view from space is changing. Now the fires burning the rainforests can be seen, new areas of desert are visible, and more topsoil can be seen building up in the river deltas. Man is changing his environment, but not for the better, and in the process he is threatening all forms of life including his own.

Four Disasters

Since I first visited Florida in the early 1960's, I've wanted to live here. My jobs and then a business kept me shivering through winters in the midwest, tantalized by the occasional escape to Florida's subtropical comfort. Vacations, visits to Mom, and infrequent business trips only increased my desire to live here, and my frustration with living up north. When, after nearly thirty years of this erratic quasi-migration, my business was sold, my thoughts and plans turned toward a big and final move south.

Arriving at last in 1990, I began to see Florida through the eyes of a resident rather than a visitor. As my blood thinned out and the warm weather became routine rather than a sporadic luxury, I tried to learn more about my new home state. I began to get off the interstates, and explore away from the tourists' beaten paths. That took me into the center of the state — away from the saltwater, the condominiums, the waterfront homes, and the shopping centers.

Where I live, on the west coast below Sarasota, going east means driving into cattle ranchland — once forests of slash pine and palmetto. Not far south of here, going east means driving into swamps and into the Everglades, the biggest shallow, grassy river in the U.S.. Only above Tampa is central Florida dotted with many communities. My drives into the hinterlands instructed me well in the environmental difficulties facing Floridians in the 1990's.

Like any populous state, Florida has the usual difficulties with automobile exhausts, solid waste disposal, sewage treatment and water supplies. As trying as some of these problems are, they are worse in many other states. To my mind, none of the above constitute major environmental problems when compared with those on my own hot list of four Florida environmental disasters — all associated with our stomachs and how we feed them.

Wait, someone will shout, how can water not be a major problem? Already many communities restrict car and boat washing. My response is that Florida has a bountiful supply of fresh water but it permits the large majority of its water to be used by agriculture rather than to be processed into drinking water for the population. The water shortages we hear about are not about supply, they are about priorities in the use of a large supply. Remove the political stranglehold of agriculture on water use, and Florida would have more water to drink than a population triple the present number would need.

Which brings me to the first of my hot list of Florida environmental disasters — beef cattle. I promised at the beginning of this book not to write a teaching book, but I can't avoid mentioning the huge amounts of water needed to produce beef. It is drunk by cows, soaked up by the grains used to fatten them, used to flush away animal wastes from feedlots, poisoned by the chemicals used to raise the grain cattle eat, etc. John Robbins totes up 2500 gallons per pound of edible beef—that's 625 gallons needed for producing a McDonald's Quarterpounder! I was amused and saddened simultaneously back on Earth Day when we were all given hints about putting a brick in the toilet tank and flushing less often to save water, but no one publicized the water content of the beef we eat. Avoiding one hamburger a year saves more water than a brick in the toilet tank. Carried to a logical end, beef means real thirst for real people.

My drives across the state through ranchland are constant reminders of the mind boggling inefficiency of creating food in the form of animal meat. And water is only one aspect. Beef production is a huge waster of energy, and clearing land in support of beef production has hurt the coastal climate, as I touched on earlier. Ranching cattle also contributes to global warming, topsoil loss, and defoliation along our rivers.

Another in my top four Florida environmental disasters is phosphate mining. Phosphate, Florida's biggest export, is mined in open pits in Central Florida. Driving on the back roads around Mulberry east of

Tampa will convince even the least environmentally sensitive of us that something is radically wrong. Giant mountains of diggings make a flat terrain look hilly, as they lay bare of vegetation in the hot sun. Huge cranes and draglines tower over the horizon, visible many miles away in all directions. Radioactive tailings are left for future generations to worry over. Processing plants and trucks keep the air full of smoke and dust. And over on the coast, ocean freighters wait to haul it all away, quietly dripping oil out of their bilges and into the fragile marine ecosystem of the Gulf of Mexico.

Phosphate is a fertilizer — a chemical we have learned we can spread on the ground to excuse the farmer from the more sustainable practices of crop rotation and contour plowing. Using phosphate, a farmer can get a quick increase in his profits, but only at the hidden cost of gradual degradation of his most precious asset—the land. Seems like sniffing cocaine — quick good times finally locking you into a loss of health, money, everything. In a real sense, phosphate destroys not only Florida's environment, but participates in the destruction of farmland all over the world. And every bit of it is used to grow crops for people and, increasingly, crops for fattening meat animals.

Sugar makes my top four disaster list. Drive over near Lake Okeechobee and see the sugar cane fields reaching to the horizon. Huge trucks rumble throughout the countryside hauling cut cane all year long. Processing plants gobble the cane night and day as the sugar industry slashes, burns, replants, slashes, burns — endlessly. What chemicals do they use? Ask an expert, not me. Some, though, have accused the sugar industry of wholesale killing of life in the Everglades through chemicals in their runoff water. The Everglades sit immediately south of sugar country.

Water collects in Lake Okeechobee and flows to the sea through the swamps to the south. Huge tracts of these swamps have been drained, irrigated, and turned into cane fields. Whatever leaches out of those reclaimed lands and whatever chemicals are applied to them eventually flow through the Everglades, a grassy river only inches deep covering nearly the entire southern tip of Florida. I can't prove who is responsible for the loss of life on the Everglades, but if this were a mystery novel, the sugar industry would be my chief suspect.

My musings over sugar are made even more ironic knowing the U.S. sugar sugar industry wouldn't exist at all without the special import barriers our government has raised to keep out cheaper foreign sugar. Talk about hidden taxes. Every time we buy sugar or anything sweetened with it, we pay extra to protect the U.S. sugar industry and perpetuate its environmental consequences.

The last disaster in my top four isn't usually seen on a drive inland. It is commercial fishing. Every day as I drive on the causeway to and from my island home, I pass a small commercial fishery. Fishermen base their small wooden boats there at night and sweep our costal waters and bays with their nets during the day. A net gets everything in its path, and you can watch the fishermen throw back what they don't want as they take in their nets. Sounds harmless, doesn't it? The unwanted fish just swim away. But the pelicans give the lie to that idea as they gather around the boats at reeling in time. They know many of the throwbacks are already dead, easily plucked out of the water by the swimming birds. They paddle over like ducks and consume the luckless junkfish, killed by the nets.

A pelican can only fish by flying and diving. The only fish he can eat while sitting on the water are dead fish. The audience of birds the fisherman plays to as he takes up his nets are really stark reminders of the waste of life in commercial net fishing. Even the sport fisherman looks askance at his commercial counterpart. He knows needless killing of small fish means fewer big fish for him to catch.

The little fishery I pass is as quaint as any scene in this part of Florida. Its metal roof, rusting in the sun, covers nets and tanks and crates of ice and shades rugged workers clad in checked shirts, denim pants, and rubber boots. It's the kind of place you snap a picture of to take back to Columbus, Ohio and keep in the end table drawer —a visual snippet to prove the old Florida lives on in isolated patches. But the snapshot doesn't show a refrigerated truck sitting outside the picturesque fishery, its diesel motor grinding endlessly, as box after box of mullet roe are forklifted onboard to be exported to Japan as a delicacy.

Does robbing our bays of mullet eggs hurt anything? Again the pelican answers for us. In these parts he has built only half the number of nests he did a few years ago. Is it only a coincidence that mullet are a mainstay in the pelican's diet? Slowly the bureaucrats are beginning to react to the commercial fishermen and rein them in. I'm hoping their oversight doesn't prove to be too little and too late.

And so you have it, my own personal top four environmental disasters here in my home state. Not the usual ones you hear about in Philadelphia or Cincinnati, but the big ones down here in palm tree country. Largely hidden from the urbanites clustered along the coasts of this peninsula, these attacks on the Earth and the life on it go on year after year with far less opposition than they deserve. They are perpetuated not only by the businesses, big and small that operate and patronize them, but by all of us through the ways we eat. Even crop eaters such as myself consume food fertilized with phosphate. Far worse, however is the environmental pressure applied to the Earth by those eating animal based foods.

I know I won't live to see a world of vegetarians, but after another hundred years of human life on Earth, no one will fail to understand the species survival imperative of a vegetarian lifestyle.

SECTION SEVEN

A FINAL WORD

Vegan Life

On a beautiful spring day I stood on Fountain Square in Cincinnati in the heart of the downtown district during the noon hour. The square was full of lunch hour lingerers who peopled the surrounding tall buildings during working hours. Tables and booths ringed the square, set up by a couple of dozen organizations with messages appropriate to the first anniversary of the second major Earth Day. This Earth Day was not the media event of the previous year; it was quieter and smaller — more of a reminder of the pledges and resolves we made twelve months before. Our organization, the Cincinnati Vegetarian Society, held forth with literature and conversation for anyone who walked by and showed interest. If someone in the crowd would slow his pace and start to study our posters, one of us would step out, offer a brochure, and say something like, "May I tell you about the Cincinnati Vegetarian Society?"

We'd done well on this Earth Day kick off Thursday — about 200 brochures were gone and a dozen people had been told where they could buy a copy of *Diet for a New America*. A young man in a business suit was asking me questions about what it's like to be a vegetarian. "Why do people become vegetarian?" he asked, and I ran through a list of reasons. For me personally, I explained in answer to another question, it was a combination of health and animal issues. His noncommittal look changed to a hint of aggression, and he said, "If you don't want animals to be killed for food, aren't you being hypocritical wearing leather shoes?"

Surprised by his stalk and pounce tactics, I guessed he was one of the thousands of Procter and Gamble suits who drone away their lives in a huge complex of buildings they call their world headquarters about three blocks away. I have always thought of those buildings as neo-Nazi architecture. I suspect those guys are all well indoctrinated about the "threat" to their way of life represented by the animal rights movement (and of course we all know most of those animal people are vegetarians). Maybe from this young man's point of view we were a threat somehow. Most of us vegetarians are not pleased about the thousands of animals they use in product testing attested to by the filings they are required to make, and who knows how many mice and rats and other little creatures they use for which no reports are required? And certainly he was aware of how consumer pressure had already cured a number of large companies like Avon, Revlon, and Bennetton of their animal testing sickness.

I smiled and said, "Look, these shoes were bought before I became a vegetarian, and it seems a lot more sensible to me to wear them out than to pay some large company to pollute the world to make me another a pair out of plastic. I don't buy leather anymore." He muttered something and moved off, his momentary lapse of smug superiority now replaced with some new thoughts on shoes. I watched him walk away thinking about the hostility he carried into a brief encounter with an utter stranger.

It was easy to be ready with an answer to his challenge, I've heard it so many times before. If I'm wearing non-leather shoes that look like leather, I just make sure the challenger knows what they're made of and that I don't buy leather any more. I spare those people the discussion about using up my old leather items. While the young man in the square may indeed have been defensive about his company's animal exploitation, challenges to a vegetarian about his shoes, whatever they are made of, are usually not about shoes or leather or animals — they are usually about the challenger's fear of living without meat. Their line of reasoning is if they can get a vegetarian to feel guilty or appear inconsistent about his leather shoes, then, as meat eaters, they can feel superior. This silly game of "gotcha," repeated ad nauseam, rarely makes a vegetarian feel guilty about anything and does nothing to diminish the demonstrated superiority of his diet. As a rule, the only thing it accomplishes is to show how little the challenger knows about trying to live a life of demonstrated compassion for animals.

I have been calling myself a vegetarian or total vegetarian meaning I don't eat any foods from animals including honey and gelatin. I will never buy wool or silk again, but I have a few items of clothing made from wool or silk I expect to wear out as I am doing with the leather shoes. Except for two pairs of shoes and a car with leather seats, I have consumed no leather since I became a vegetarian. The car is gone and the latest has fabric upholstery. I don't expect to buy another new car with leather, and I hope I can avoid buying leather shoes again, but in this one area, I find the non-animal substitutes lacking. Either you show up at dinner parties wearing canvas or you wear leather substitute shoes and look like you just got off the boat. For men at least, the world of non-leather shoes is a small, not well designed one. Charlene has great looking non-leather shoes with a leather look in nearly every color. Ladies shoes like this are available in most of the big shopping centers.

I pronounce vegan with a long e and a hard g accenting the first syllable, and so do most of my friends. My doctor and some others use a short e and a soft g. No matter how you say it, vegan means to attempt life without exploiting animals directly or indirectly. Here the word "attempt" is required because it is not possible to live absolutely without consuming some of the results of animal exploitation. Andrew Linzey, the Anglican minister, who has worked so hard for a better Christian ethic toward animals has said, "There is no pure ground," meaning that some vestige of animal exploitation can be found in all our lives. It is, unfortunately, ubiquitous.

Did you take an aspirin recently? How many animals have been used testing aspirin? Any prescription drug has likely been tested on animals as well as most household products. There are animal products in automobiles and on them in the form of the wax we use to shine them. Animals are exploited for the movies we watch, trained dolphin and whale shows, at every zoo, and in most carnivals. Precisely because there is no pure ground, I think status as a vegan must flow first from one's spiritual commitment to avoid exploitation and second from his track record in doing so. Every backsliding, like that car and those shoes I bought, should not serve to cancel one's status, but rather as a reason to strengthen one's resolve to do better in the future. For myself, I go on haunting shoe stores looking for the imprint saying, "all man made materials."

The American Vegan Society, an organization I respect, seems to define vegan as abstaining from animal source food or clothing. I think perhaps "abstain" is too harsh in that it would require me to throw away clothing bought in may preveg days rather than to use it up. On the other hand, I think "food and clothing" is too narrow because so many other animal exploiting products exist in our society. I believe the magazine, *Vegetarian Times,* suggested dietary vegan to describe someone who eats no animal foods, but doesn't avoid leather, wool, etc. We can go on and on cutting these definitions closer, but in the end it isn't organizations and publications which define terms in our language — it is generally accepted usage. When someone tells me he is a vegan, I know he cares about animals and does the best he can to avoid consuming animal products. That is more important to me than whether he might have an old wool sweater stuck away in a drawer or a leather wallet his mother gave him in his pocket.

Charlene's license plate in Florida is GO VEGAN, a great license plate message. I wish many more people knew and used the word and practiced the life. For my part, I'm trying, and I hope you are too.

SOMEWHERE A HEART BEATS

I saw a pig
Climb a truck ramp slowly
On three legs.
We crippled him,
And he still did his best for us.

Do we think that if we eat their bodies
We will have their strength?
Do we think that if we kill them
We will have their life?
Do we think that God closes his eyes
After we say grace?

And if we break his heart,
What will be left in our own?

-Betty Jahn